FRESHMAN ORIENTATION

House Style and Home Style

Edward I. Sidlow

Eastern Michigan University

CQ PRESS

A Division of Congressional Quarterly Inc.
Washington, D.C.

CQ Press
1255 22nd Street, N.W., Suite 400
Washington, D.C. 20037

Phone: 202-729-1900; toll-free, 1-866-4CQ-PRESS (1-866-427-7737)

Web: www.cqpress.com

Photo credits: CQ Press, *Politics in America 2006,* front cover; Laurie Tennent, 52, back cover; Trumpie Photography, 140

Cover design: Tony Olivis

Text permission: "The City of New Orleans," written by Steve Goodman. Published by Jurisdad Music o/b/o itself & Turnpike Tom Music, 32

⊗ The paper used in this publication exceeds the requirements of the American National Standard for Information Sciences--Permanence of Paper for Printed Library Materials, ANSI Z39.48-1992.

Printed and bound in the United States of America

10 09 08 07 06   1 2 3 4 5

ISBN-10: 1-933116-65-X
ISBN-13: 978-1-933116-65-5

The Library of Congress CIP data is available under Library of Congress Control Number 2006038176.

To the memory of my mother

Contents

Preface

IN THE EARLY 1980S, when I was a much younger faculty member at Miami University, a student who had taken every class that I taught remarked to me as he neared graduation, "I'll always remember your classes...you told such interesting, funny stories about politics." My teaching assistant was in my office at the time, and I saw her smile at my discomfort over what the student thought was high praise. Later, as we walked to class together, she said, "C'mon, let's go tell a few good stories." I mumbled something about viewing them as illustrations, examples, maybe even lessons; but she was too busy laughing at my annoyance and celebrating how easily she had gotten under my skin to hear what I was saying.

As a young political scientist, I found this sort of evaluation troubling. I was, after all, trained to be a university professor, not a storyteller; I felt then that storytelling lacked the requisite seriousness of purpose for an appropriate academic posture. Over the years, though, it has, thankfully, become easier to take myself less seriously. I now realize that if my goal is to teach, and if stories bring material to life for my students, then maybe being applauded for telling stories well is not, after all, a sign of academic weakness.

This book tells a story. I think it is an interesting one, and I hope I have told it in an engaging way. I have taught classes on congressional politics for nearly thirty years but have always wondered how a member of Congress manages to put together staff operations in two different places, organizes multiple offices, and learns the rules of the legislative game all at the same time. I assumed it had to be exhausting but had not found much in the literature that connected real people to this arduous process. Simply stated, I wanted to observe the congressional socialization process and was happy to find a willing subject in Joe Schwarz, a physician who was seeking the Republican Party's nomination in my home congressional district in Michigan. I knew that the experience would inform my teaching in classes on legislative politics, but I also suspected that there might be a good story or two in it.

I started following Joe around in the summer of 2004, as he ran in the Republican primary for a seat in the U.S. House of Representatives in Michigan's Seventh District. Joe won that election handily, and I followed him to Washington, D.C., for his first days on Capitol Hill. From the inauguration of the 109th Congress through the elections of November 2006, I stayed in regular contact with the Schwarz operation, visiting with the congressman in Washington or with his staff in Michigan at least once a month. I also met with Joe on some of his many trips back to the district, and I went to Washington when there were functions on his schedule that could illustrate the varied aspects of a congressman's workload. Finally, I observed various events in the campaigns that the Schwarz team ran in 2006.

The election season of 2006 offered up one additional and very timely lesson. As most readers who follow politics closely already know, Schwarz, a moderate Republican, ended up losing his bid for reelection in the bruising Michigan primaries in the summer of 2006. In the final chapter I place Schwarz's experience in the broader context of the tumultuous 2006 election season.

The events reported in this book are based on observation, interviews, and secondary source data. Press accounts of relevant material and some nationally archived election data help to tell a more complete story. While meeting with the congressman or his staff, I always carried a microcassette recorder equipped with an internal microphone, along with a ready supply of batteries and unused tapes. I recorded my own observations as well as answers to questions that I posed to those involved in the events of the moment. At various times, I conducted lengthy interviews with the congressman, his staff, and members of the congressman's inner circle. Frankly, I took my opportunities when they were available. To label this approach a "methodology" is generous, but I am nonetheless indebted to Richard Fenno, whose pathbreaking work has made it easier to produce this kind of volume and to have it find an audience in our discipline.

The crux of this story is the learning curve of a new member of the House of Representatives. The Schwarz example illustrates the processes of hiring a staff and dividing up the considerable workload of any congressional office. It also examines many of the relationships that a member of Congress must cultivate to be effective in such a complex work environment. The successes and frustrations of an actual congressional office, as well as some of the pace of congressional life, are described in a way that, hopefully, resonates with readers. I have tried to humanize the congressional operation so that students—and, perhaps, a more general audience—can recognize that real people make real sacrifices to undertake public service. This book also offers a glimpse into the campaign industry of consultants, political pros, and fund-raisers that has become such a vital part of politics in the twenty-first century.

My training as a political scientist helps me to place the Schwarz operation in a broader context and to highlight the behavioral patterns to be expected from members of congress, their staffs, and others with whom they interact in the circumstances that arise throughout the story. Moreover, the work benefits from, and is informed by, decades of scholarship by political scientists around the country. Consequently, the conclusions and generalizations that I make throughout this book are steeped in theoretical and analytical material that is at the heart of our basic understanding of American politics.

I have incurred many debts while working on this project. Peggy Burns of the University of Michigan facilitated my initial introduction to Joe Schwarz. The Office of Research and Graduate Studies at Eastern Michigan University (EMU) provided a grant in support of research, for which I am most grateful. Also, my Undergraduate Honors Fellow, Micheal Balke (2005–2006), helped with indexing and analyzing data from public records and with transcribing tapes for the project. Friends and colleagues provided support and encouragement for which I am also very grateful. Among them, Mike Beck took an interest in the project from the beginning, and we managed to meet when we were both in Washington in the spring of 2005. He has no idea how much seeing a friendly face in the midst of fieldwork for this kind of project can pick up a guy's spirits. Barry Pyle, my colleague at EMU, proved a thoughtful sounding board and helped to ease the balance of writing with teaching and other university obligations.

Obviously, this work could not have been done without the generosity of Congressman Joe Schwarz. Joe was always willing to make time for me, and he took me along to a variety of meetings that allowed for extraordinary access to the work world of the House. Matt Marsden, chief of staff for the D.C. office, and Rebecca Schneider, district director in Michigan, were good-spirited in putting up with my phone calls, questions, and the general nuisance that I was throughout the project, and I am very grateful to both of them.

The Schwarz staff was uniformly helpful, generous with their time, and tolerant of my snooping around. Chuck Yessaian helped me to schedule trips at fruitful points in the year and kept me in the communications loop among the Schwarz offices. He also was patient with the many "quick questions" that often turned out to be anything but quick. Schwarz staffers in Washington and Michigan—including Faye Armstrong, John Berg, Rob Blackwell, Paul Egnatuk, Robert Glazier, Jeane Johnson, Meghan Kolassa, Louie Meizlish, Cheryl Nebbeling, Jared Page, Dawn Saylor, and Aaron Taliaferro—were all very welcoming; without their help, this story could not have been told.

Alison Dagnes, Shippensburg University; Christine L. Day, University of New Orleans; Stephen R. Routh, California State University, Stanislaus; and one anonymous reviewer all provided welcome insight and motivation, and I thank them for their thoughtful comments.

Brenda Carter, Charisse Kiino, and Elise Frasier, all of CQ Press, have been an absolute pleasure to work with. They quickly grasped what I wanted to do in telling this story, and their input has greatly improved the work. Elise and I spoke frequently, and, as was the case in our past collaboration, she remained a steadying influence on the project. Katharine Miller was also a joy to work with, and the book surely benefited from her deft copyediting. My thanks to Anne Stewart as well for her able handling of the production of the book.

Throughout the process of writing this book, my daughter, Sarah, has managed to keep me focused on what's really important. As the book was in its last stages, she was completing her first season of high school varsity tennis. There were days when tennis matches took precedence over writing, and I thank her for that. I hope I kept my eye on the ball as well as she did. My wife, Beth, made rough prose smooth and was always there to help in the midst of juggling professional obligations and family responsibilities. She also managed to teach important lessons, both inside and outside the classroom. She's fond of the declaration of a psychologist friend of ours: "We're always teaching." Indeed, she is.

Finally, while I was doing the fieldwork for this book, in the summer of 2005, my mother passed away. It is to her memory that this book is dedicated.

E. S.
Saline, Michigan
October 2006

Prologue
Election Night, 2004

"No, DAMMIT, I don't want any exit poll bullshit. I want real numbers."

Matt Marsden, campaign manager of the "Schwarz for Congress" campaign, stood at the end of a conference table, barking orders to what looked like a team of college kids. Matt, a thirty-two-year-old political consultant, like so many other campaign directors working behind the scenes for elected officials, was feeling the adrenaline rush that is palpable in every campaign war room on every election night.

I smiled to myself, thinking, "Here we go again. Another story about politics...and the people who make politics fun and interesting."[1] I was following Joe Schwarz, a candidate for the U.S. House of Representatives for Michigan's Seventh District, who was himself an interesting story. An ear, nose, and throat doctor who had also served in the Michigan state senate and had been mayor of Battle Creek, Schwarz would turn sixty-seven shortly after the election, and if he won, he would certainly be the oldest member of the new congressional freshman class. (Still, he would be a long way from the oldest freshman congressman in history; that distinction belongs to William Lewis of Kentucky, elected to the House in 1946 at the age of eighty.)

Also, I would have a willing subject, who would let me watch and record the congressional learning curve as it unfolded—the exciting, and often painful, "freshman orientation" that brand-new members experience every time a new session gets underway in Congress. As a university professor, I was used to seeing "real" freshmen participating in the various campus programs designed to acclimate them to undergraduate

1

life, but observing a congressman during his first year in office would reveal a rather different kind of freshman orientation. Instead of learning how to find their classrooms, freshman congressmen must find out where the committee hearing rooms are; their assignments involve placement on standing committees and subcommittees, as opposed to papers and exams. One other big difference is the lack of a syllabus that tells a freshman congressman what the class can expect.

The election night activities were being held at Win Schuler's Restaurant in Marshall, Michigan. Schuler's is a family-run, destination restaurant that is an institution in lower Michigan, situated about halfway between Detroit and Chicago. It is a wonderful old place with murals depicting "historic Marshall, MI" on the walls and memorable sayings—such as "Facts are stubborn things. –Rene LeSage" and "One man with courage makes a majority. –Andrew Jackson"—etched into the beams on the ceiling. The restaurant's current owner is Hans Schuler, who represents the third generation in the family business, and whose friendship with Dr. Schwarz is so old and so deep that it made perfect sense to all who know them that his place would host this election night gathering, which, if all went well, would later become a victory celebration.

A private room at Schuler's was set up for supporters, staffers, campaign volunteers, and well-wishers. Television sets all around the room offered wall-to-wall news coverage of the Bush-Kerry presidential race, but the front of the room was reserved for a podium adorned with a "Schwarz for Congress" banner. There were buffet tables and a bar, balloons, and all the trappings of an election night gathering. Radio and newspaper reporters from nearby Battle Creek and Jackson also showed up, as did a couple of television news crews.

Up a flight of stairs from the party room was the election night "war room," where members of the campaign staff gathered around a conference table cluttered with phones and four laptop computers. The preferred source for up-to-the-minute returns was www.campaignmagic.com, though various state and county Web sites were also checked frequently. There was some tension in the room, but also an air of anticipation. The "Schwarz for Congress" team expected to win—their real fight had come during the primary election back in August. It was much too early to start talking about claiming victory, but the early returns looked very promising.

The following chapters chronicle the story of how a new congressional office is set up and how a new member of Congress goes about learning and doing his job. We cover issues as serious as the "right to die" and the proper role of government in the business of embryonic stem-cell research, and as unexpected as the need to remove the mold covering an office wall and presenting a health hazard to Hill staffers.

We also examine how representation happens—or doesn't—and how a congressman divides his time between Washington and the home district, and between a Washington office and three district offices. This story, like the life of a member of Congress, is unpredictable, exhausting, and at times exhilarating. Along the way, finally, we observe the making of public policy as it plays out in Congress.

Michigan's Seventh
Congressional District, 2004
The Primary Season and the Candidates

MICHIGAN'S SEVENTH CONGRESSIONAL DISTRICT, which is shaped a little like a rectangular piece of a jigsaw puzzle with an off-center top hat, stretches across the lower-middle portion of the state's lower peninsula. It contains all or parts of seven counties, two of which border northern Ohio and one that touches Indiana. Busy I-94 runs through the district and serves as the primary roadway between Detroit to the east and Lake Michigan and Chicago to the west. The landscape presents a mixture of small towns and rural areas, though there are some small cities of note within the district.

Nearly at the center of the district lies the city of Jackson, which is credited with being the birthplace of the Republican Party. The party name, basic political platform, and initial organization were put together there on July 6, 1854, at a gathering of roughly three thousand people who sought to promote a single cause—the abolition of slavery. Once a station on the Underground Railroad, Jackson retained a reformist flavor, evidenced by local support for women's rights, Prohibition, and opposition to the death penalty in addition to its very early opposition to racial segregation.

Battle Creek, Michigan—best known as birthplace to the American breakfast cereal industry—is about an hour west of Jackson, at the western edge of the Seventh District. During the late 1800s, Dr. John Kellogg was instrumental in building a health sanitarium in Battle Creek, where he and his brother, W.K. Kellogg, developed and later marketed a cereal they called "granola." The Kellogg Company and the W.K. Kellogg

Michigan's Seventh Congressional District

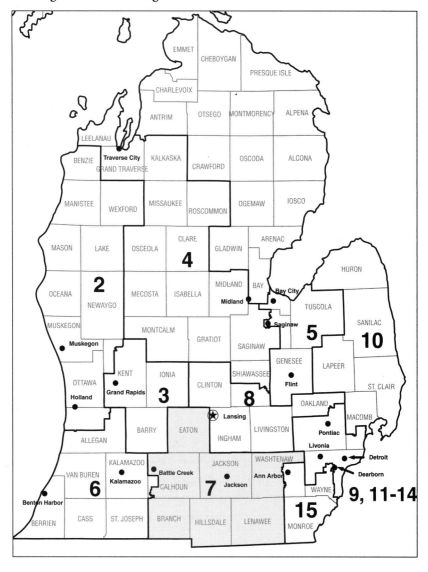

Foundation are still very much a part of the local scene. Interestingly, C.W. Post, founder of a competing cereal company, was also from Battle Creek; he was inspired to found his company after receiving treatment at Dr. Kellogg's sanitarium. Post Grape Nuts was his first cold cereal, introduced in 1892. Battle Creek takes its cereal heritage seriously.

Adrian (in Lenawee County, near the southeastern corner of the district) and Albion (in Calhoun County, about midway between Jackson and Battle Creek) each house liberal arts colleges that bear the cities' names. Siena Heights University, another small four-year institution, is also located in Adrian. The Seventh District includes a piece of Washtenaw County, home to the University of Michigan in Ann Arbor and Eastern Michigan University in Ypsilanti, but neither of these campuses is contained in the district. The district lines also come very close to the Lansing area—home to Michigan State University—but this major institution lies in the adjacent Eighth District. Nevertheless, many Seventh District residents are employed by these major educational institutions, and many more have children attending them. Given these connections, in addition to the several institutions of higher learning that are located within the district's own boundaries, it is no surprise that education is an important constituent concern.

Since 1992, the Seventh District has been considered safe for Republican congressional candidates, and it is best described as having a largely conservative constituency. In previous years, however, the district had a distinctly different character. Until 1992, the city of Flint was part of the Seventh. Made famous by the Michael Moore movie *Roger and Me*, Flint was one of the largest "company towns" in the United States; highway billboards welcomed you to "Buick City" until the 1980s brought hard times to the American auto industry. During its heyday, Flint had five major General Motors plants, and GM employed more than half of all of Flint's families. The blue-collar population of Flint made up the largest bloc of Michigan's Democratic voters outside of metropolitan Detroit.

In 1966 Donald Riegle was elected to the House from the Seventh District as a moderate-to-liberal Republican. Not always popular with his fellow Republicans, Riegle enjoyed the support of typically Democratic groups such as the United Auto Workers (UAW), blacks, and local anti–Vietnam War peace organizations. In 1973 Riegle switched parties but kept his House seat—as a Democrat—until 1976, when he was elected to the U.S. Senate.

From 1977 to 1992, the district was represented by another popular Democrat, Dale Kildee, who was known for his personal, door-to-door campaigning. Kildee experienced the unusual success of passing legislation as a freshman when he initiated the measure that ultimately made producing child pornography a federal crime. In 1992 redistricting—carried out by a federal court when both the Republican and Democratic plans for redrawing the congressional lines were deemed too partisan—took Flint and its heavily Democratic voting bloc into the Fifth District, where Kildee has consistently won reelection. That removal, meanwhile, left the Seventh District overwhelmingly Republican, consisting of voters in the agricultural areas, towns, and small cities that characterize it today.

The elections of 1992 brought Republican Nick Smith to Congress as part of the largest freshman class since World War II. His arrival came in the middle of a period of upheaval (1990–1994) during which 194 members retired from the House and 112 others lost their bids for reelection. Those combined figures represented a turnover of 70 percent in three elections, while the normal House turnover is about 10 percent per election. In 1994 Smith would be joined by 73 Republican freshmen, who, along with Speaker Newt Gingrich, were to have a profound effect on the nature of congressional politics. This group entered the House in a period of strong anti-incumbent sentiment, fueled by House banking and post office scandals as well as by voter discontent with a bad economy. During his campaign, Smith pledged to serve no more than twelve years. After winning reelection with relative ease during the following five election cycles, he honored his commitment and retired from the House in 2004. During his time in office, Smith maintained a consistently conservative voting record.

When Smith stepped down, the Seventh District became an open seat, and, as it turned out, the prize of a heated and tumultuous Republican primary campaign. It was expected that the seat would remain Republican, given the demographics of the district, and thus that the winner of the party's primary on August 3, 2004, would be the district's next representative.

Given the rarity of open seats in House elections, it was not at all surprising that the Republican primary field was crowded in the summer of '04. The candidates included five conservatives, among whose positions on the issues there was little difference, and one moderate, who was easily distinguishable from the rest of the pack. As political strategists rightly suggested, this race presented a perfect set of conditions for a bunch of like-minded candidates to split the votes of their supporters.

Conservative candidates Clark Bisbee, Gene DeRossett, Paul DeWeese, and Tim Walberg had all served in the Michigan House of Representatives. Fellow conservative Brad Smith, a successful attorney with a large, well-known law firm, had clerked in the U.S. Court of Appeals for the Fifth Circuit in the mid-1990s, but he had no political experience. As the son of Rep. Nick Smith, he was, however, seen by many as the heir apparent to the seat his father had held for the past dozen years.

The lone moderate in the crowded primary field was Joe Schwarz, whose political experience included service both in the Michigan state senate and as mayor of Battle Creek. A physician who continued practicing while holding office, Schwarz had served in the navy in Vietnam and later worked for the Central Intelligence Agency.

In late June, the Associated Press characterized the Republican primary in the Michigan Seventh as a race between Joe Schwarz, "a John McCain-style Republican," and five other more conservative Republican candidates. The AP story also noted that it was very difficult to determine any issue differences among the conservative group.[1] Indeed, there was agreement across all six Republican candidates regarding the war on terror and the invasion of Iraq. All supported the Bush administration's positions on these politically linked undertakings and were aware that this twofold issue was not only on the minds of voters in the summer of 2004 but was also likely to absorb a fair amount of the congressional agenda on which all of them hoped to be working. There was, however, no such across-the-board agreement on the other major issues of the day.

One issue that all of the candidates were asked about during the campaign was the ban on assault weapons that Congress had passed in 1994, during the Clinton presidency. The ban was set to expire at the end of 2004 if Congress failed to renew it. Bisbee, DeRossett, DeWeese, Smith, and

Walberg all indicated that they would vote against renewing the ban, while Schwarz claimed that he would vote to extend it. In a profile of the candidates that ran in the *Battle Creek Enquirer,* each was asked to state his position on abortion politics. Once again, Schwarz stood out from the crowd as the only candidate to support a woman's right to choose. The other candidates stated that, if given a choice, they would "vote to overturn the *Roe v. Wade* decision that legalized abortion."[2]

The differences among the candidates were more nuanced when it came to economic issues and domestic government spending. In a Republican candidate debate held on June 30, Smith declared that "whole programs should be eliminated." He claimed that he "would support repealing the new Medicare prescription drug law and consider doing away with the National Endowment for the Arts and the U.S. Department of Education." DeWeese and Walberg announced that they "would eliminate the Internal Revenue Service and replace the income tax with a consumption tax." And, as the *Lansing State Journal* reported, "Bisbee, Smith and Walberg all said they would make a no-tax-increase pledge," while the other three candidates said they would seek to avoid tax increases but would make no iron-clad pledge. Schwarz indicated that Congress should reduce pork-barrel spending, but he was once again distinguished as the moderate member of the Republican field.[3]

Two Schwarz campaign staffers, twenty-nine-year-old Paul Egnatuk and twenty-five-year-old Mark Ratner, noted that the campaign was not the least bit shy about playing up the differences between Schwarz and the other candidates. As Mark put it, every Schwarz speech contained an underlying element of "... there's me, and just to the right of me there's Attila the Hun, and then on the right side of Attila, there are these other five guys that I am running against." Paul traced another distinction between Schwarz and the other candidates—a "geographic split," as he described it:

> Draw a line from Lansing near the top of the district through Jackson at the bottom. All five of the others live east of Lansing and Dr. Schwarz is the only one on the west side of the district... and he's from Battle Creek, the largest city in the district. Wait... Paul DeWeese tried to palm himself off as being from Eaton Rapids, which is west. But actually, he worked in Eaton Rapids and acquired an apartment there after he started running.

He honestly didn't live in the district. The other five candidates, in some respects, were splitting up the same geographic vote as well as the same ideological vote.

For the Schwarz team, one of the most noteworthy events of the primary campaign was a two-day visit by Senator John McCain (R-Ariz.) to stump for his friend Joe. A Republican Party celebrity, McCain drew significant crowds and media attention wherever he traveled. Furthermore, he lent serious credibility to any candidate he supported.

Senator McCain and Joe Schwarz had become friends during the 2000 presidential campaign, when Michigan was hotly contested in the Republican primary period. George W. Bush relied on Governor John Engler to deliver the state for him, and, in fact, it was reported that Engler had promised to do so. Many assumed that if he succeeded, and if Bush then won the White House, there would be a cabinet post waiting for Engler in the Bush administration. McCain's Michigan operation was directed by Joe Schwarz, then president of the Michigan state senate.

Winning the Michigan primary would be a significant prize for either candidate, for McCain had scored a surprise victory in New Hampshire a few weeks earlier, while Bush had won the South Carolina primary the previous week in one of the dirtiest campaigns of the primary season. Michigan was the first of the industrial states' primaries, and both candidates felt they had something to prove. In the election, McCain pulled out a stunning victory, winning 50 percent of the primary vote, to Bush's 43 percent and Alan Keyes's 5 percent. Although McCain ultimately did not win the Republican nomination, he did attract substantial support in the 2000 primary race, and the Michigan experience certainly added to his stature as a national political figure. Moreover, it helped to cement the relationship between McCain and Schwarz. Their friendship should be no surprise—both are decorated Vietnam veterans, both are seen as moderate Republicans, and neither is afraid to take issue with the party leadership.

The McCain visit in 2004 produced some very special moments and, not surprisingly, generated a fair amount of press. The Schwarz team had planned a two-day bus tour, during which their candidate and Senator McCain would make four different appearances together on the first day

Joe Schwarz and Senator John McCain had become friends during the 2000 presidential primary season, when Schwarz directed McCain's successful effort in the Michigan primary. In 2004 Schwarz was clearly delighted to have McCain's support in his bid for the House seat from Michigan's Seventh District.

and seven on the second. Since many Republicans, including President Bush, were routinely asking him to stump for them, McCain's time was precious, and so the campaign team thought it was impressive that the senator—of whom Schwarz once remarked, "He's the closest thing we have to a national hero"—was willing to give two days to stump with a challenger during the height of the 2004 campaign season.

Around noon on Friday, July 16, campaign staffers picked up McCain at Detroit Metro Airport, which is a couple of hours east of the Seventh Congressional District. The first event on the schedule was an annual summer festival, called "A Taste of Battle Creek," which typically draws throngs of people to the center of town—to listen to bands performing on outdoor stages and enjoy the typical hoopla of summer weekend events in towns across America. According to the Schwarz team's plan, a band on the main stage was to introduce McCain, who would, in turn, talk up the Schwarz candidacy and then introduce Dr. Schwarz.

Anybody who has worked on a campaign knows that sometimes things do not go according to plan, and any Midwesterner knows that summer weather can be fickle. In the late afternoon of July 16, 2004, Battle Creek was engulfed by torrential rain. Mark Ratner described the scene:

> This was supposed to be a big deal, but it was just pouring. The campaign bus still showed up, but instead of a big crowd, there were about 100–150

people in a big tent. Well, the two of them just walked into the tent. Dr. Schwarz climbed up on a picnic table and started introducing Senator McCain. No microphone, no introduction of the candidate, just Dr. Schwarz projecting loudly in his public speaking voice, really just sort of yelling a few words about McCain. Then, McCain gets up on the table and just wows the crowd. It was great. It literally had the feel of an old-fashioned stump speech. Real genuine.

Following the rain-soaked "Taste of Battle Creek," the bus rolled on to Lansing, where Schwarz and McCain taped a campaign commercial together and then went on to the retirement party for a woman who had worked for Eaton County for thirty-five years. As Paul Egnatuk tells it, "They invited Dr. Schwarz because he had been a state senator and he knew many of the Eaton County government folks. Of course, she had no way of knowing if he would come or not, given that he was in a heated primary election campaign battle. So he shows up to this lady's retirement party with John McCain. As you can imagine, that just floored her." From the retirement party, it was off to the Eaton County Fair, where Schwarz and McCain walked around greeting people.

Lt. Joe Schwarz pictured here after his first tour of duty in Vietnam, 1966. The picture was taken in Jakarta, where Joe was stationed for a time as a naval attaché.

Stops on the following day included a business start-up in Bellevue, a small town in the southwestern part of the district. There was another visit to Battle Creek, and then it was off to Branch County, the northernmost county in the district—this time for the annual Polish festival in Bronson, a town of about 2,500. Next, a major event at the Jackson Airport featured a hot-air balloon show and appearances by members of the Tuskegee Airmen, as well as by Joe Schwarz and Senator McCain. After a stop in Adrian, the tour ended in Saline, a small city near Ann Arbor, where McCain and Schwarz spoke to a good-sized crowd from the expansive front porch at the home of Rebecca Schneider, who had known Schwarz for several years and was helping with the campaign.

It had been a memorable two days of activity, as the Schwarz campaign staffers hustled to make the most of the buzz generated by McCain's endorsement. They had every reason to hope that the prominent senator's tour of the district with their candidate, appearing at the festivals and rallies and fairs that are so much a part of the landscape of American electoral politics, would contribute to a victory for Joe.

As the weeks of the primary season wore on, the race for the Republican nomination continued to reflect the ideological differences between Schwarz and his five opponents. The ultraconservative candidates seemed to pay little attention to the economy, health care, jobs, or national security, focusing instead on social issues. As Paul Egnatuk observed, they wanted to make the race about "abortion, gays, and guns"—issues on which Joe Schwarz took comparatively moderate positions. "It was frustrating that they kept calling Joe 'pro-abortion,'" Paul noted. "It was a calculated misrepresentation of his views." With the exception of one substantive debate, on the topic of health care, between Schwarz and Paul DeWeese (who, like Joe, is a practicing physician), there was little discussion of the issues that were drawing attention at the national level. Instead, Schwarz found himself challenged by some nasty insinuations and negative ads.

One ad, in particular, angered many in the Schwarz campaign organization. Toward the end of the primary race, a Tim Walberg ad intimated that Schwarz would support giving a valid driver's license to terrorist Osama bin Laden. Walberg claimed that as a state senator, Schwarz had taken a position making it easier for illegal immigrants to obtain licenses in Michigan. Mark Ratner still bristles at the thought of that ludicrous charge:

> Joe did support a measure in the state senate that would have made it easier for migrant workers who were here legally to get a driver's license. But turning that into allowing illegal immigrants to get licenses is just not true. In fact, the bill specifically addressed the issue, with language making it clear that "this bill does not allow illegal immigrants to obtain drivers licenses."

Negative ads, of course, are nothing new in the world of politics. As scholars of electoral politics have noted, whether the prize be the top job in the nation or one seat in a chamber of 435, mudslinging is a feature of most professional election campaigns—and one that plenty of campaign professionals believe actually wins elections.[4] Regardless of the likelihood of bin Laden's taking up residence surreptitiously in Michigan, therefore, Walberg's campaign wanted it known that Joe Schwarz could be held personally responsible for allowing the master terrorist to drive on the state's highways.

As the day of the Michigan primary drew closer, the race seemed to tighten. The leading contenders were Brad Smith, son of the incumbent congressman, and Joe Schwarz. The final phase of the primary race brought with it a fair amount of drama, some of which had been foreshadowed a year earlier.

On November 22, 2003, the House of Representatives had voted on the Medicare prescription drug bill supported by the Bush administration. The measure passed by an extremely thin margin—and only after the House floor had been kept open for three hours while the Republican congressional leadership struggled to win over Republican members who had initially opposed the bill or who were leaning toward voting against it. One of those Republican holdouts was Nick Smith.

In a radio interview shortly after the House vote, Congressman Smith claimed that he had been offered a bribe to support the Medicare drug bill. Specifically, Smith said, he had been promised $100,000, as well as national Republican Party endorsements for his son's 2004 campaign to represent Michigan's Seventh District, if he would join the leadership and vote for the bill. When Smith declined the offer, declaring that he was "going to stick to my guns on what I think is right for constituents in my district," the bribe became a threat; his refusal to vote with the leadership was met with the following response from the Republican leadership: "If you don't change your vote … there's some of us who are going to work to make sure that your son doesn't get to Congress."[5]

The entire matter resulted in a House Ethics Committee probe, as well as a Justice Department investigation. It also received considerable attention in the national press. Covered at various times by CBS News, CNN,

Joe Schwarz, head in hands, at one of the many Republican candidate forums in the run-up to the August '04 primary. Joe's posture here may well indicate his exasperation at what he called the "absolutist views" of his Republican primary opponents.

USA Today, and the PBS *News Hour,* among other media outlets, the story was kept alive through the spring and summer months while the 2004 primary battle back in the Michigan Seventh was being waged. Ultimately, the Ethics Committee "publicly admonished" both Majority Leader Tom DeLay (R-Texas) and Rep. Candice Miller of Michigan's Tenth District, for ethics violations in the episode.

Amid the swirling story of the ethics investigation stemming from his father's claims on Capitol Hill, Brad Smith was experiencing financial issues of his own. In late July 2004, a month before the primary, the Schwarz campaign filed a complaint with the Federal Election Commission, charging Smith with violation of campaign finance laws. The allegation was that Smith had loaned money to his own campaign in an amount that made him ineligible for the increased campaign contribution limits that are reserved for candidates who do not or cannot substantially fund their own campaigns. Schwarz, who had relatively little of his own money invested in his campaign, was thus eligible to receive contributions in larger amounts from individual donors. His campaign charged, however, that Smith was not.

The League of Conservation Voters ran an ad on a Lansing television station claiming that "Smith had broken the law" by accepting illegal campaign contributions. Another group also criticized Smith in TV and radio ads for raising so much money from outside the district and questioned whether he might be influenced by external interests if he were to be elected. In response, Brad Smith claimed that he was being falsely accused and hammered Schwarz for being too liberal to adequately serve the constituents in Michigan's Seventh District. As election day approached, headlines in the *Battle Creek Enquirer* announced, "7th Congressional Race Is Heated for GOP" and "Candidates Continue with Last Minute Ad Wars."

On a very warm primary night, August 3, 2004, the Schwarz team gathered in the small meeting room of Schuler's restaurant. The staffers in the war room all remember the atmosphere as hot, sweaty, and intense. Paul Egnatuk recalls, "We didn't have a very good system for tracking results at that point, and people were just yelling out numbers...that really didn't help ease the tension at all.... It was quite an adrenaline rush."

At about 11:00 p.m., while the radio and television stations were still reporting the race as "too close to call," the numbers the Schwarz team was seeing made them start to think that they had won. By 11:30, the vote results were coming in quickly over the Internet. When officials in Hillsdale County reported their results, it became clear that Smith could not catch Schwarz, and the mood grew festive. There was a good deal of back-slapping, high-fiving, and hugging, and, about ten minutes after the Schwarz team was sure that they had won, the candidate went downstairs to claim victory. The final results showed Schwarz with 28 percent of the vote; Smith with 23 percent; Walberg with 18 percent; Bisbee with 14 percent; and DeRossett and DeWeese with 7 percent each.

It had been a tight race and a tough campaign, but now thoughts had to turn to the general election in November—just three months away. Paul remembers how he felt just after the primary victory:

We made it through. ... We had the celebration, dismantled the 'war room,' popped all the balloons...this was about an hour or so after we

Taking his campaign to the people, Schwarz bought advertising on a dirt-track sprint car competing at Butler Motor Speedway in Branch County, Michigan.

were certain. ... Then we went to the bar. I remember sipping a beer. ... I was just plain exhausted. The euphoria lasted about half an hour. ... I also remember rearranging the office a couple of days later, cleaning up some stuff from the primary campaign, and thinking to myself, "This could have gone the other way, and we could be cleaning this place out for good, rather than just rearranging it for the next three months."

Of his victory, Schwarz said he felt "great and relieved." He was pleased that his campaign "did not pander to people who are obsessed with moral absolutist social issues and was able to succeed by appealing to a broader cross-section of voters." Upon learning of his victory, Schwarz called his friend, Senator McCain, and chatted with him for several minutes, happily accepting the senator's warm congratulations. In his mind, the major political battle had been won, and, as he put it, if he could just "keep on keepin' on," things would go well in November.

Shortly after the winning the primary, Dr. Schwarz took some time to visit his place in Montana, on land that he and his late wife had purchased in the 1970s. Joe's wife had come from Montana, and the place and its memories remained very special to him. Although he managed to find time to go there toward the end of each summer, it looked particularly inviting after the primary election of 2004. The trip allowed him to take a breather for a couple of days before beginning to make specific plans for the fall's general election campaign.

Because the Seventh District is so overwhelmingly Republican, the Democratic primary received far less media attention. It featured Drew Walker, a forty-one-year-old businessman who had returned to his native Battle Creek after years of living in New York and abroad; Douglas Wilson, a forty-year-old paramedic who actually lived outside the district, but who promised to relocate if he won the primary; and Sharon Renier, a forty-eight-year-old organic farmer. While Renier had made an unsuccessful run for the state legislature in 2002, neither Walker nor Wilson had sought public office before. Walker trumpeted his support from local Democratic officials, while Renier hoped to hold onto the support she had been able to build during her run for the statehouse two years earlier. As for Wilson, some people were left, as a Jackson newspaper put it, "scratching their heads why the Oakland County resident is running in a district in which he doesn't even live." [6]

In this low visibility primary, Sharon Renier handily beat her two opponents, garnering 58 percent of the vote; Walker and Wilson got 22 percent and 19 percent, respectively. In fact, Renier won a majority in all seven counties in the district while spending the least amount of money of all the candidates competing in either party's primary. Running what she called a "people's campaign," Renier didn't put up a single yard sign. Instead, she spent most of her funding—about $2,000—on a thirty-second ad that ran on public television in Jackson County. Even she was surprised by her margin of victory, but she recognized that it would be an uphill battle against Schwarz in the general election.

2

Open-Seat Battle
Electing a New Member of Congress

ONE OF THE great paradoxes in American politics is the contrast between the high level of interest and intensity brought to a congressional election campaign by those involved in the process, and the bored indifference that characterizes most voters' views of the race. As Paul Herrnson has pointed out, "Most voters make their voting decisions on the basis of relatively little information. ... In open seat House contests, about 37 percent of all voters can remember both candidates' names."[1] That two-thirds of the voters will not remember the candidate's name can be demoralizing to many young staffers and campaign workers. In House elections, voters tend to respond most strongly to a couple of cues: the candidate's party affiliation and whether an incumbent is running. In an open-seat election—such as the contest between Joe Schwarz and Sharon Renier in 2004—partisanship serves as the dominant factor in voters' response.

Given that Michigan's Seventh Congressional District had been comfortably Republican since the 1992 redistricting, the partisanship cue would certainly work to Schwarz's advantage. Although Al Gore had carried Michigan in the 2000 presidential race, for example, George W. Bush had won in the Seventh District, garnering 51 percent of the vote there. (Four years later, the Democratic presidential candidate, John Kerry, would win the state, but President Bush once again prevailed in the Seventh, this time with 54 percent of the vote.) Thus it was widely expected that the nominee who emerged from the Republican Party's bruising primary would likely be the victor in November, and most political observers agreed that the Seventh was Schwarz's to lose in 2004.

This is not to say that Schwarz had no competition. Open seats do attract candidates, and as had been the case in the primary, the field in the general election was crowded. In addition to Schwarz, the Republican, and Renier, the Democrat, the race included a Libertarian Party candidate, Kenneth Proctor; a candidate from the U.S. Taxpayers Party, David Horn; and Jason Seagraves, representing the Green Party.

In a presidential election year, of course, the race for the White House is uppermost in the minds of the voters, and other electoral contests usually take a back seat. In 2004 President Bush and Senator John Kerry were engaged in a very heated, highly visible race, and both spent a great deal of time in Michigan, since the state was seen as a "toss up," which either candidate could win. Moreover, Michigan's proximity to Ohio, considered a key battleground state, meant that Bush and Kerry were often within striking distance of Michigan while campaigning in the Buckeye State. Both presidential candidates, as well as their running mates, Vice President Dick Cheney and Senator John Edwards, campaigned in Michigan on numerous occasions. And, because there was no senatorial or gubernatorial race in the state in that year, there were no statewide media buys—coordinated purchases of TV or radio commercial time in every media market in the state—except those made by the presidential campaigns. What little publicity there was concerning congressional elections got lost in the din of the battle for the White House.

The general election campaign in the Michigan Seventh thus presented different challenges than the heated primary race that Schwarz had just won. Staffer Mark Ratner noted that, this time, it was difficult to keep focused. Ratner, who had graduated from Michigan State University with a degree in political science and had worked for Schwarz during his last term in the state senate before being hired as part of the campaign team, explained, "There was so much outside stimulus pushing you in the primary—opposition coming at you from multiple candidates and campaigns on a daily basis. ... It was absolutely impossible to suffer from over-confidence at that time. The general election presented other problems." Mark observed that he was genuinely concerned about complacency in the Schwarz camp:

> You don't want a sleeper like Sharon Renier to jump up and bite you. ...
> Look at what she did. With virtually no money she managed to beat
> two candidates quite handily in her primary. She won over 50 percent of
> the vote in a three-person field. You can't ignore that. I think she raised the
> money for her first campaign event in the primary by picking up and
> redeeming soda and beer cans and bottles that she collected from the side
> of the road. As light as she was on funds, she managed to win, and I kept
> reminding myself not to lose sight of that.

Paul Egnatuk, a University of Michigan graduate who had interned for
Schwarz during his college days and had left a job in the construction
trade to work on the 2004 campaign, also expressed concern about keeping focused and about not becoming overconfident:

> We kept our candidate's schedule as busy as possible. ... We kept running ... but I found it difficult with everybody on the outside telling us
> "it's in the bag." Frankly, that added more pressure, of a different sort. I
> kept thinking, "Boy, if we manage to screw this up, we're in big trouble."
> And the pressure was subtle, and probably self-imposed. ... You know,
> you get a call from a reporter who says, "Look, I'm doing a story on this
> race and I need a few minutes with Joe. I know you've got this thing won."
> And I'm busy thinking, "Please ... don't say that ... that's not my attitude at
> all. ... I'm not assuming that in the least."

In effect, Paul and Mark and their colleagues working on the campaign
had to find a way to avoid appearing cocky, while at the same time not
disingenuously pretending to be concerned. A nice problem to have, certainly, but it meant that the Schwarz staff had to keep their guard up,
while also living with the imbalance of worrying about their own local
race for Congress while the rest of the country—and, so it seemed, the
world—focused on President Bush and Senator Kerry.

Matt Marsden, Schwarz's campaign manager, was dealing with other
concerns during the general election campaign. Though in his early thirties, Matt appeared ageless. After graduating from the James Madison

College of Michigan State University, Matt had begun his political career in 1996, in the mail room of Michigan Governor John Engler, and soon moved to the Communication Division, where he worked directly for the governor's director of communication and press secretary, John Truscott. Matt started doing advance work for the governor—that is, arranging for public appearances and seeing to the vast number of details involved in preparing for an appearance by a political leader. The job included site selection for a political event, advertising, insuring that a crowd of voters would be in attendance, making press credentials available, and planning for the arrival and exit of the public official around whom the event was planned. He helped to plan the first visit that George W. Bush made to Detroit, before his presidential campaign was officially launched, and then went on to do advance work for the White House after Bush was elected. Matt's work for the president took him all over the country and abroad. In fact, he was with President Bush in Florida on the morning of September 11, 2001, when the World Trade Center and the Pentagon were attacked by terrorists. At the suggestion of his former boss John Truscott, Matt came to work for Joe Schwarz in the spring of 2004, bringing a wealth of experience, an aptitude for multitasking, and a wonderful sense of humor to the Schwarz campaign.

Matt, like other campaign professionals, worried about money. While Mark Ratner and Paul Egnatuk were keeping the candidate's schedule full and trying to draw attention to the race in the Michigan Seventh, Matt was focused on a peculiar fund-raising problem. When the campaign's fund-raiser, Jennifer Bertram, approached people who were considered quite likely to contribute to the Schwarz campaign, she would often be met with an attitude that implied, "Hey, you're going to win anyhow. Why should we give you money?" Matt realized, of course, that money was still needed to pay the staff, rent the offices, and cover the telephone bills, printing, gas, yard signs, and myriad other expenses of campaigning. As he explained,

> Despite what the public perception of a race is, you need a lot of things to keep a general election campaign operational. We had to go to the big donors and say "Look, we need you to give the maximum allowable, $2,000 per person in a congressional election, and we need you to organize

and host fundraisers." I am very grateful that they came through for us—at times it seemed like a tough sell, but our supporters were great, and that's certainly a tribute to Joe.

Matt's former boss John Truscott was also playing a role in the Schwarz-for-Congress effort. The consulting firm he had opened after leaving Governor Engler's administration was now retained by the Schwarz operation to provide campaign guidance and management advice. Truscott, too, was concerned about fund-raising. One of the ironies of campaign politics is embedded in the very essence of the relationship between campaign professionals and the candidates for whom they work. While the candidate is the "boss," the campaign pro is responsible for telling the candidate what he or she is doing wrong. As odd as it may seem, the campaign professional gets paid for yelling at the boss—more evidence that politics is a weird business.

Truscott, who took his work very seriously, was not shy about showing his displeasure with his candidate-client, Joe Schwarz. He did not hesitate to fire off a highly critical email in early September 2004, chastising Joe for some comments he had made at a gathering. Apparently, at a fundraising event that was running late, Joe had told folks to feel free to leave if they needed to—and about half the group left. "Are you avoiding the ask for dollars?" Truscott's email accusingly inquired. (In campaign jargon, "the ask" is a candidate's specific and pointed request for donations.) And that was just the opening salvo. The page-long email continued:

> On the fundraising front, you're not making any of your calls. People are working their tails off to raise $300,000 for the general and can't do it alone. This is also a sign to potential opponents two years from now. If you go back into the old mode of not being willing to raise money, that does not bode well for two years down the road. We did a good job [in the primary] of blowing up the perception that you don't work hard and you don't like to raise money—but this is not a gimme. ... We still have $40,000 in debt that we're carrying—we were barely able to make payroll last week, especially since you gave everyone raises—and hired a new person and won't let Matt get rid of anyone. The payroll is very high and there were some unexpected expenses that crept in on us. ... We're under 80 days to go, but trust me, this whole cycle will start back up in January. This

general election campaign is more about two years from now than it is this November. You will have two years of constant campaigning and fundraising. If you show weakness at any time, it will invite opposition. Please don't pull a Spence Abraham.* You have too much to offer.

Truscott's point was not lost on Dr. Schwarz. When the campaign concluded, there would be a nice cushion of cash on hand to be carried into the 2006 election season.

As the campaign rolled through the fall, the Schwarz team participated in all of the standard activities that typify a run for elective office—parades, street fairs, coffee hours, and fund-raisers. Joe continued to see patients at his medical practice, although that diversion became, at times, a source of scheduling frustration for his staff. Nevertheless, the mood was generally up-beat and positive.

One particularly noteworthy event took place on September 13, 2004, when President Bush, on a several-day bus tour of Midwest battleground states, planned a campaign stop and rally in Battle Creek. Joe Schwarz was scheduled to speak, as was the out-going congressman, Nick Smith. The site chosen for the event was C.O. Brown Stadium, then home to the minor league Battle Creek Yankees. The Schwarz group all planned to meet at the campaign office in Battle Creek and head over to the event at about 1:45 p.m. Joe arrived late—he had been tending to his medical appointments—but, somewhat to his staff's dismay, took control the moment he walked through the door. A few days earlier, Danielle Moreland, a member of the campaign staff, had arranged for a police escort to the stadium for Joe and his party. Joe's car would be parked right next to the grandstand on the ballpark grounds. The whole plan had been cleared through the president's Secret Service detail, which took care of security in and around the stadium during the president's visit. But when Matt Marsden told Joe about the arrangements as he entered the office, Joe immediately nixed the plan. "We're not doing that," Joe decided. "If we

---

*The reference to Spencer Abraham is telling. Abraham was a one-term U.S. senator from Michigan who lost his 2000 reelection bid to a two-term House member, Debbie Stabenow. That defeat was particularly stinging to Republicans because they managed to retake the White House from the Democrats in that year.

park that close to the stadium, we'll never get out. We're going to park about 15 minutes away and walk in."

After a flurry of cell phone conversations between Matt, Danielle, and the local police, a route was approved for Joe to take to the stadium. Joe laughed at all the carrying on, slid behind the wheel of his Ford Explorer, and proceeded to ignore the suggested route. He drove on back streets, through various neighborhoods, and parked the car in a convenience store lot. Along the three-quarters-of-a-mile walk to the ballpark, Joe was greeted by literally hundreds of people. Many knew him from his days as mayor of Battle Creek or as a state senator, and others had been or still were his patients.

About two blocks from the stadium, Joe's group reached a police barricade, through which no one was permitted to proceed until the Secret Service was satisfied that the grounds were secure. A call was placed to Danielle, who was inside the stadium as part of Joe's advance team, and she soon arrived at the barricade, accompanied by a very large Secret Service agent, to vouch for Joe's group so that they could enter the grounds. Joe remained good-humored about the delay, using the time to visit with other folks who were waiting to be admitted to the rally.

Presidential events often involve the distribution of a variety of tickets in different colors, each color representing a different level of proximity to the president. Of course, the most prized tickets allow those who have them to be closest to the president or along the "rope line," which may afford a handshake with the chief executive as he enters or exits the event. Danielle was holding a number of tickets in all colors, and Joe's immediate group was seated at the very front of the venue.

A country music group entertained the crowd for a time, and then the speeches began. Joe spoke with enthusiasm about the accomplishments of the Bush administration and the need to reelect the president; he also offered criticism of the president's rivals. In return, President Bush thanked Joe, and asked the crowd to support Joe and other Republican candidates in November. He then gave a standard stump speech heralding what had been achieved during his first four years in office and painting his opponent—he refused to acknowledge John Kerry by name—as a "flip-flopper" and tax-crazed liberal from Massachusetts. The partisan crowd cheered wildly, and the president, in his folksy way, thanked everyone for coming as he left for his next campaign stop.

Later, at a reception at the Arcadia Brewery, a micro-brewery in Battle Creek that is owned and operated by a friend of Joe's, there was plenty of friendly banter, as people wished Joe well over cold beer, pizza, chips and salsa, and the like. Joe, however, admitted that he was uncomfortable with the speech he had given, explaining, "The president's people asked me for a rally-the-troops kind of red-meat speech, and that's just not my style. I am much more comfortable with reason and compromise than I am with that kind of bash-the-opposition speech. You'll never hear me give that kind of speech again." Joe's predicament illustrates the president's influence on congressional politics—even during the preelection stage.

The reception was crawling with local officials and politicians. With a sarcastic grin, Matt mentioned that he looked forward to having all those who had fought him so bitterly during the recent primary season "making nice-nice" to him and asking for jobs on the Schwarz campaign. As if reading from a script, a woman who had been part of one of the opposition teams in the primary appeared at Matt's elbow, offering congratulations in a most ingratiating way. It was a wonderful example of the strange mating dance of politics: she wanted a job, and Matt wanted the donor lists from her campaign operation. When the conversation ended, Matt smiled and said, "That's politics. The stores are always open, 24/7."

The day after the president's visit, Joe and Matt were off to Washington, D.C., for three days of meetings. While the campaign staff would continue to say that they were taking nothing for granted, it was clear on the inside that they expected to win in November. That expectation was bolstered by the fact that several interest groups in D.C., as well as a number of congressional Republicans, were eager to meet with Joe.

One of the groups that Joe and Matt were scheduled to visit was the Republican Main Street Partnership. Sometimes referred to as "the Mainstreeters," this group claims to have been "founded in 1998 to promote thoughtful leadership in the Republican Party, and to partner with individuals, organizations and institutions that share centrist values."[2] The group's membership constitutes a virtual "who's who" of moderate Republicans, including Joe's friend John McCain, and several of McCain's

Senate colleagues, including Lincoln Chafee of Rhode Island and Susan Collins and Olympia Snow of Maine, and a few dozen House members, including Mark Kirk of Illinois, Chris Shays of Connecticut, and fellow Michiganians Fred Upton, Vern Ehlers, and Dave Camp. If he were to win in November, Joe would fit in with this group and be welcomed by them.

Matt was blunt about one of the purposes of this trip to Washington. "One thing we're gonna do," he said, "is to stop by the Republican Congressional Committee and pick up some money." Given the uncertain outcome of the primary, the National Republican Congressional Committee had wisely stayed away from the Seventh District in Michigan until that contest was settled. Now that Joe Schwarz was the Republican candidate, the campaign arm of the Congressional Republican Caucus was eager to see him win in November. The trip to Washington also included courtesy visits to several Republican members of Congress and meetings with business, conservation, and transportation interest groups, among others.

The Schwarz team pressed on through September and October, keeping its candidate as busy as possible and doing all that they could to remain visible in the din of the highly publicized—and, at times, quite bitter—presidential campaign. There were frustrations, often brought on by Joe's insistence on seeing patients at his medical office in Battle Creek when the campaign team would much rather have had him somewhere else. Overall, though, things appeared to be going smoothly.

On Monday, October 4, a debate—billed as a "candidate forum"—featuring all five candidates for the House seat was held on the campus of Siena Heights University in the town of Adrian. Sponsored by the local newspaper, the *Adrian Daily Telegram*, and the American Association of University Women, the debate followed a standard format: a panel of media types asked questions of the candidates, and there was time at the end for questions from the audience of about 150. Like most such events around the country during election season, the debate featured some thoughtful dialogue, some contentiousness, some humor, and some strange statements. In other words, there was something for everyone.

The Schwarz staff had not made any special preparations for the debate, since Joe felt that he was well-versed on the major issues and did not find such events the least bit intimidating. The first issue raised at the forum was the war in Iraq. Most of the candidates supported the war effort, some less passionately than others. Schwarz said that there was no point in discussing whether we should be involved in Iraq, because "the fact is, we are there . . . and because we are there, we must fulfill our obligations there. . . . We've got to give our troops everything they need, we've got to give the Iraqi government everything it needs, and we've got to find an appropriate exit strategy." The closest position to an antiwar stance came from the Libertarian candidate, Kenneth Proctor, who declared that American troops should leave Iraq on July 4, 2005, and announced that he was opposed to a military draft, which he viewed "as a form of slavery." Jason Seagraves of the Green Party allowed some uncertainty about the war but stated, "America should not serve as the world's police force." [3]

The death of President Reagan four months earlier had brought stem-cell research to the foreground as a political issue. Reagan's widow, Nancy, and their son, Ron Jr., were very public in their support of this new field of research, believing that stem-cell technology might have helped in the treatment of the former president and that it held promise for others who suffer from Alzheimer's disease. The typical conservative position was opposition to stem-cell research; thus Nancy Reagan's support for it was welcome in moderate and liberal circles. It came as no surprise, then, that stem-cell research was raised as a topic in the debate.

Joe Schwarz is passionate when talking about embryonic stem-cell research, expressing his professional opinion as a physician that its potential is valuable and that it must be pursued. He is quick to tell any listener that "you cannot argue about the science in stem-cell research," but equally quick to say that he will not step on others' personal convictions, although he believes that many people are misinformed on the subject. He has said on numerous occasions, "I will not argue with anybody's moral or religious beliefs, but I will not allow anybody to argue the science of embryonic stem-cell research with me." Schwarz's command of the subject was on display for everyone to see and hear during the debate. When David Horn of the U.S. Taxpayer's Party said that he opposed stem-cell research because "one life should not be traded for another," [4] he was quickly dismissed by Schwarz. In a state of near-exasperation, Schwarz countered, calling stem-cell research "a fact of life." Clearly, his medical training put him on firmer ground to discuss the issue than most of his opponents.

Not surprisingly, abortion was another topic of discussion during the candidate forum. Seagraves, of the Green Party, favored abortion rights, claiming, "Women are not slaves to men or the state and should not be told what they can do to their own bodies."[5] Proctor, the Libertarian, indicated that while his party supported abortion rights, he was personally opposed and thought a solution to the abortion dilemma might be found in embryo transfer. (This suggestion seemed to confuse some in the audience, while amusing others.) Horn, of the U.S. Taxpayer's Party, and Democrat Sharon Renier both said they were personally opposed to abortion. Renier, however, also stated that she would not support overturning the Supreme Court's decision in *Roe v. Wade* (1973), which is at the heart of the national debate over the abortion issue. For his part, Schwarz was animated on the subject. After noting his personal opposition to abortion, he explained that he would, nonetheless, strongly oppose any effort to reverse *Roe*. "We will not return to the pre-*Roe* days in this country," he declared emphatically. "As a medical doctor, I have seen the work of butchers and back-alley abortionists, and any return to those days is unacceptable."

Joe Schwarz's status as the front-runner in the campaign was clear during the candidate forum. He behaved as if that was the case, and the deference shown him by the other candidates added to the perception that he was the man to beat. His preeminence was also obvious from the audience reaction and from the crowd that gathered around Joe at the conclusion of the evening. Joe's staffers were confident and more than satisfied with how the evening had gone as they left the campus auditorium and headed home.

As the campaign wound through October, there was no shortage of people from various organizations who wanted to meet with Joe. On October 19 Joe and Matt met with representatives from Amtrak—Ray Lang was director of the rail service's Government Affairs Division, working out of Chicago, and Steve Matson was a foreman based in Pontiac, Michigan. They met Joe and Matt at the Ann Arbor station to begin a train ride from east to west across the Seventh District to the station in Battle Creek; the train was to stop in the towns of Dexter, Chelsea, and Jackson along the way.

This particular train had a "head end," five passenger cars, and an engine in the back. Absolutely fascinated by trains, Joe had loved them since he was a boy, when his father would take him to the Battle Creek station so that he could watch the trains come in and leave again. The candidate was all smiles as he shook hands with the engineer, a big, burly fellow with a bushy gray beard—straight out of central casting. Joe Rafferty had worked on the railroad for 28 years but had 108 years worth of stories, and Joe Schwarz appeared eager to hear every one of them. But this was not just a pleasure trip, for the Amtrak officials had done their homework. They knew that if Joe were to be elected, they would have another friend in Congress—and Amtrak could use all the friends it could get. The congressional appropriations process has a major impact on Amtrak's budget, and recent history had not been kind to Amtrak.

The day was gray and overcast, but as the train wound its way through Washtenaw County along the Huron River, the fall landscape offered eye-popping shades of yellow, red, and orange. The scene conjured up the lyrics to a Steve Goodman song, popularized by Arlo Guthrie: as the train "rolls along past houses, farms and fields…mothers with their babes asleep, are rockin' to the gentle beat and the rhythm of the rails is all they feel."[6] About ten minutes into the ride, after introductions and pleasantries, Rafferty said to Schwarz, "I understand you are an Amtrak supporter and I'm grateful for that, but Joe, how does it look for my job for about the next ten years?" The response was direct and to the point. "Well," Dr. Schwarz replied, "I'm going to do everything that I can to keep it and protect it." No more business had to be conducted. Amtrak officials had made their point, and Joe Schwarz had made his.

While Rafferty had Joe's attention, however, he used the opportunity to press other issues. "Hey," Rafferty called out, "there's something else. You've got to help us hunters. The Canadians aren't letting us in for duck hunting…and we've got to get that taken care of. It all has something to do with our imports of Canadian cows, and you've just got to deal with that." Schwarz chuckled and said he would do what he could.

The Amtrak folks had "goody bags" for Joe and Matt that included safety glasses—needed when walking through the empty space between the passenger cars and the "head end"—tee shirts and other trinkets, and Amtrak literature. The candidate responded by demonstrating an impressive knowledge of the railroad. He explained that this line, built to follow the rivers, was once the main line for east-to-west travel through Michigan. He pointed out businesses along the way, and indicated that he knew most of the people who ran those businesses from his days in the state senate.

As the passengers commented on the physical beauty of the landscape, the train pulled into the Jackson station, and Rafferty was reminded of a previous trip. "You know," he ruminated,

> there are times along this route that you hit things…animals. Trains are not nimble like automobiles, and if something is sitting on the track… well, there's not much you can do. One time, when I was pulling into the Jackson station, I remembered having hit a couple of wild turkeys along the way. When we reached the stop, as passengers were getting on and off, I went out and pulled a dead turkey from under the front of the train. I put it aside, and when I got to my home back in Battle Creek, I took it with me, skinned it, and cooked it.

Rafferty was laughing at this point, and Schwarz shook his head, saying with a chuckle, "Well, that's the mark of a real man—a guy who will eat his own road kill." Everybody had a good laugh. Sensing that he had a willing audience, Rafferty continued, "That was some of the chewiest, toughest meat I've ever had in my life. I should have cooked it differently." He paused. "No, wait a minute…the moose ribs I had from a moose I killed in Alaska were tougher than that wild turkey!"

The train ride was fun—politics at its most pleasant. It also illustrated just how many different characters and situations candidates come across as they campaign for Congress.

The Schwarz team was clearly pleased to see the newspaper endorsements start rolling in during the month of October. The *Ann Arbor News* endorsed Schwarz in an October 13 editorial that began, "Republican is best choice for 7th District," and concluded, "Schwarz, we're convinced, would make a difference for the 7th District."[7] On October 24 the *Delta Waverly Community News* strongly endorsed Schwarz's bid for Congress, editorializing, "It is hard to imagine a better potential Congressman than Schwarz, who would arrive in Congress as an expert in governing, health care issues, the military, and higher education."[8]

Dr. Schwarz was also supported by the *Lansing State Journal,* and, on October 24 he received a ringing endorsement from his hometown paper, the *Battle Creek Enquirer.* The piece in the Battle Creek paper began,

> Many of the decisions facing voters on Nov. 2 will be difficult, but in the race for Michigan's 7th Congressional District, there is one candidate who clearly is the best qualified to go to Washington, D.C.: John "Joe" Schwarz. ... As a local physician, former mayor and four-term state senator, Schwarz has demonstrated not only a commitment to this community, but an ability to stand up for what he believes is in his constituents' best interests and fight to ensure that they receive a fair shake.[9]

The Schwarz campaign also was delighted to receive the endorsement of the *Detroit Free Press,* the paper with the largest circulation in the state.

On election night, the Schwarz team was back at Win Schuler's Restaurant, and the same war room that had been a beehive of activity on the sweaty August primary night came alive once again. This time, however, the Schwarz camp expected to win. The atmosphere was looser than on primary night, and the party room downstairs was filled with smiling people who paid attention to the presidential election on the televisions placed around the room and who hoped to be among the first to congratulate Dr. Schwarz on his victory.

In the restaurant's main dining room, the candidate himself was having dinner with his family. Joe's thirty-year-old daughter Brennan, who holds a masters degree in public policy from the University of Michigan, and who works as a policy advisor to the House Republican Caucus at the Michigan statehouse in Lansing, was at the table. So, too, was Joe's sister Janet, a retired schoolteacher who makes her home in Battle Creek. They were joined by Joe's brother Frank, a retired physician who had traveled from his home in New Mexico to be with the candidate on election night, and by Joe's good friend Hans Schuler. The mood was happy, though anxious.

Meanwhile, upstairs in the war room, the campaign staffers—Matt Marsden, Paul Egnatuk, Mark Ratner, Louie Meizlish, Danielle Moreland, and Rob Blackwell—gathered around five laptops feeding off a wireless router. Matt was in control, and he wanted voting returns. He refused to look at exit poll data. On this night, Matt knew his candidate was going to win—the question was by how much. Matt had set a personal goal of 60 percent of the vote, which would be a comfortable margin of victory and go well beyond President Bush's 51 percent of the district in 2000.

By 10:00 p.m., the staff members were comfortable that the votes were there for Joe and that they were truly at a victory party. But some of the counties were slow to report, and Joe wanted to wait until votes were reported from every county—he did not want to run the risk of alienating any county clerks by declaring victory before they reported their specific vote totals. At about 11:00 p.m., Joe spoke to the crowd, indicating that the numbers were looking good but that it was still too early to say that he had won. Finally, though, shortly before midnight, to the delight of his staff, family, and friends, a tired but happy Joe Schwarz offered his thanks to all of them, claimed victory, and vowed to do his very best to represent the wishes of the Seventh District when Congress convened in January 2005. Around 1:00 a.m., the congressman-elect spoke to his friend John McCain on the phone, accepting the senator's congratulations. Schwarz had won with 58 percent of the vote.

On Wednesday morning, Joe met with his staff, saw a few patients in his medical office, and went through what he referred to as "eight zillion e-mails." Then he began making plans to attend "freshman boot camp," as he called it, and looking for a place to live in Washington, D.C.

Setting Up Shop

TRANSITIONS ARE DIFFICULT—both from candidate to congressman and from campaign to congressional staff. After his November victory, Congressman-elect Schwarz and his team had less than two months before the January 4, 2005, swearing-in ceremonies to make the required transitions to their new positions.

Joe Schwarz found himself one of thirty-nine—twenty-four Republicans, fifteen Democrats—newly elected members of the House of Representatives in the 109th Congress. The arrival of these newcomers on Capitol Hill, coupled with the departure of the members whose seats they had filled, set off the ritual, complicated game of "Room Draw"—or, more candidly, "grab that space." Offices now vacated would first be made available to members who had served in the preceding Congress, some of whom would choose to move to a more spacious office, or to one with a better view, leaving their old offices for the freshman class to divvy up. Then, according to custom, a lottery would be held for new members, assigning numbers to indicate the order in which they could select an office from the spaces available. Among those taking office in 2005, the member drawing number 1 had the widest choice; the member with number 39 had the most limited selection. Since Joe Schwarz had drawn number 38, he and Matt Marsden were not hopeful about the office space they would get. "When you are that far down on the list," Matt noted, "it's silly to have great expectations."

To Matt's surprise, however, a first-floor office in the Cannon Building was still available when it was Joe's turn to select his space. A first-floor location means no long waits for elevators on the way from the office to the floor of the House for votes and debate. Room 128 had been vacated by Ed Case, a Democrat from Hawaii, who had just won a second term and had decided to move down the hall and around the corner to Room 115.

The Cannon Building, which was opened in 1908 and named for Joe Cannon, the powerful Speaker of the House from 1903 to 1911, is the oldest of three House office buildings. It is situated southwest of the Capitol Rotunda, on the other side of Independence Avenue. Across the street is the Library of Congress, and a block or so away is the U.S. Supreme Court.

Schwarz's new office space, measuring about 1,000 square feet, was due to receive fresh paint and new carpeting before the congressman and his staff moved in. While the first-floor location could be seen as a plus, the space itself is a bit awkward, since the rooms are not entirely contiguous. The door to 128 Cannon opens into a small reception area, leading to the congressman's office and an adjacent office assigned to his legislative director. The closest hallway door is a women's restroom; beyond that, a door leads to the other half of the office space—a good-sized room that is partitioned off to house the rest of the congressman's staff. While somewhat inconvenient, the divided configuration does allow the staff a sense of independence, and it affords the boss a fair amount of peace and quiet. Besides, freshmen members don't have a lot of choice in these matters.

In addition to setting up his office, Schwarz had a staff to hire, his own housing in Washington to find, and a number of meetings to attend. The week of November 15th was to be spent at a series of orientation seminars sponsored by the House Republicans. Also during that week, President Bush hosted a lunch at the White House for incoming legislators. Seated next to Vice President Dick Cheney, Joe Schwarz spent an hour talking with him about a range of issues, including national security, health care, and AIDS. Joe realized that one-on-one time with the vice president does not happen often, and he was not about to fritter away this opportunity. Several obligatory dinners were also on the calendar that week. One such event was hosted by Speaker of the House Dennis Hastert (R-Ill.), and

Rep. Joe Schwarz in the corridor near his new offices in the Cannon Building. Schwarz's freshman team was surprised that he had drawn such a choice location, since such offices are typically snatched up by more senior members.

another was given by the powerful House majority leader, Tom DeLay (R-Texas).

During that hectic period in Washington, Joe also managed to find time to have a drink with a lobbyist. Of that meeting, Joe said with a grin, "We had a very serious and weighty discussion." The lobbyist, an old friend who worked for the University of Michigan Medical Center, spent his time with Joe "covering the important matter of the upcoming Michigan vs. Ohio State football game." This great rivalry typically consumed Joe on the third Saturday of November every year, and, new congressman or not, he was not about to shift his priorities. As a proud alumnus of the University of Michigan, Joe took Wolverine football seriously, and to Michigan fans, the game against Ohio State is as serious as it gets.

Of course, Joe's introduction to Washington as a new congressman consisted of more than dinners and drinks. When, on the day following his election, Joe had remarked that he would soon be heading off to what he called "boot camp for new congressmen," he was more nearly correct than one might imagine. In fact, the training process for new members of Congress (MCs) is similar in many respects to the orientation provided to most college freshmen. Newly arrived on campus, incoming students are usually given a canvas bag or backpack emblazoned with the college or university seal and stuffed with far more written material than anyone could possibly absorb in a short period of time. The barrage of information includes everything from how to get a student ID card to how to complete the paperwork for graduation. Likewise, Joe Schwarz and the other thirty-eight new House members each received a large blue canvas tote bag, on the outside of which was a picture of the Capitol and large print proclaiming "109th Congress—New Member Orientation." Just as on any college campus in the fall, these freshmen MCs could be spotted a mile away. And, just like the new college students' welcome bags, those that had been prepared for the new House members overflowed with a daunting amount of material to be absorbed in a short time frame.

The centerpiece of that information package was a large three-ring binder, entitled *2004 House Manual: New Member Orientation, 109th Congress,* which had been put together under the direction of the Committee on House Administration. The first item to be found inside, in the pocket on the back of the front cover, was a notice from the Office of the Chaplain of the U.S. House of Representatives, the Reverend Daniel P. Coughlin. The notice, printed on Coughlin's official stationery, included information about the chaplain's Web site and the location (just off the Rotunda) of the Capitol Prayer Room—"a place set aside specifically for members of the House and Senate for private reflection."[1] Instructions were given for how MCs could recommend guest chaplains, and information was provided about the weekly prayer breakfast sponsored by the chaplain's office. There was also an invitation from the Speaker and the minority leader for members and their out-of-town-guests to attend the "109th Congressional Bipartisan Interfaith Prayer Service," scheduled for 9:00 a.m. on "Swearing-In Day," January 4, 2005. Doubtless, many freshmen congressmen and congresswomen have taken a look at the stacks of orientation material in the new member canvas bag and felt that they could use some help from a higher being to digest it all.

Along with the chaplain's notice, the front pocket of the binder contained material about the Congressional Research Service (CRS), a nonpartisan entity whose assistance is available to all members of Congress, for the provision of informed research on any policy matter in which a legislator is interested. The CRS also has experts on staff to assist the MCs with procedural and budgetary matters. Located in the Library of Congress, the service has become essential to conducting legislative business.

The several hundred pages that made up the orientation binder were divided logically into sections. For example, Section 1, whose tab read "Member's Handbook," included detailed payroll information for staff and other financial matters, as well as guidelines on legitimate reimbursable expenses that members might incur while serving in Congress. Section 2, entitled "Franking Regulations," covered the congressional franking privilege, which allows members to mail material to constituents at taxpayers' expense. The practice is sufficiently complex—requiring guidelines for what kinds of material can be franked, and what cannot (such as political or campaign material)—that it was covered in a paperbound book of 92 pages, which had been produced to fit into the *House Manual* but could be removed as a stand-alone publication. A couple of examples of acceptable franked newsletters were included; while they touted the accomplishments of the member for whom they were produced in a way that might be thought of as conveying political information, these newsletters fell within the bounds of acceptable, nonpolitical mail. Suffice it to say, the frank is of considerable benefit to incumbent members of Congress, whose staffs soon learn how best to utilize it.

The binder also held sections labeled "Ethics," "Equipment Guide," "House Rules," "Model Employee Handbook," "Legal Guidelines," "Staff Classification," and "Additional Information." Clearly, this large, bureaucratic volume was important, but no one was going to be able to process all of this information during the orientation period or in the few short weeks between the elections and the swearing-in ceremonies. Indeed, Congressman Schwarz's copy of the manual is testament to the fact that

Above, Joe joins his fellow freshmen for the New Member Orientation of the 109th Congress. The thick binders before them contain information about everything from House ethics rules to how to operate some of their basic office equipment. Left, Joe logs into the House computer system at orientation.

even the most diligent of new members might be a bit distracted as he or she tried to digest the rules and regulations of the institution. And, much like a college freshman's dry instruction packet, Joe's manual shows indisputable evidence of doodling in the margins. There is a rough sketch of the state of Michigan, with the counties of the Seventh Congressional District drawn in. On another page, the letters MICH appear, in the block style that is so commonly seen on sweatshirts in Ann Arbor. Perhaps the upcoming Michigan–Ohio State game was occupying some small part of Joe's thoughts as he was being oriented to the ways of Congress. A bit of daydreaming is understandable during "boot camp."

The seminars held on Capitol Hill offered instructions on setting up a congressional office, using the House computer system, and learning how to work the BlackBerry devices that are so common in Washington, D.C. There were also lessons on ethics, committee and caucus organization, office budgets, and a host of other administrative matters. Joe likened the information overload to "trying to get a drink from Niagara Falls," but figured that most of what he was taking in would become clear when the new congressional session began and he was fully engaged with the institution and the processes that characterize it. While he was not at all intimidated by the nature or content of the information that was being presented, the sheer volume was a bit overwhelming. Nevertheless, he knew that a learning curve comes with any new job.

Matt Marsden, whose title had changed from campaign manager to chief of staff, found himself attending his own training camp while Joe was busy with his seminars. The Congressional Management Foundation, "a non-profit, non-partisan organization dedicated to promoting a more effective Congress," sponsored a program in "Setting Up Your Congressional Office," which was based on the 9th edition of its 300-page book, *Setting Course: A Congressional Management Guide.*[2] (There is no hard evidence of doodling in Matt's copies of the materials provided in this program. Given Matt's loyalty to *his* alma mater, Michigan State University, it is perhaps fair to speculate that some artwork similar to Joe's may have been created, but, shrewd political operative that he is, Matt would likely have destroyed any hint of daydreaming.)

The goal of the staff orientation is spelled out in the final paragraph of the introduction to *Setting Course:*

> In the classic 1972 film, *The Candidate,* Robert Redford portrays an idealistic young man running for the Senate against an entrenched incumbent. The final weeks of the campaign are a frantic whirl of events, and no one—not the candidate, nor the campaign team—has time for a single thought beyond election day. Redford wins, of course—this is the movies—but on his way to deliver his victory speech in the famous final scene, he pulls his campaign manager aside and asks in a daze, "What do we do now?"

Where *The Candidate* ends, *Setting Course* begins. The text covers the transition period, the process for making appropriate committee assignment requests of the party leadership, office budgeting, hiring core staff, selecting technology for the congressional operation, and establishing offices in the district. Mastering this information is critical, for staff members must know how to run the entire office bureaucracy, which necessarily involves budgetary and fiscal management, hiring and firing, and other difficult personnel issues. The nuts and bolts of the congressional office are far more important than they are interesting.

Schwarz and Marsden came away from their November meetings realizing that they had a great deal to do in order to have a fully functioning congressional operation by early January. In addition to putting things together in Washington, they needed to secure office space and hire personnel to work in the district back in Michigan. As Robert Salisbury and Kenneth Shepsle have pointed out, one of the impacts of the growth of the congressional support bureaucracy is the fact that the member of Congress has become "an enterprise," wherein the elected representative becomes the ultimate supervisor of an operation that can range from a dozen to over one hundred subordinates. Particularly dramatic expansion of congressional staffing occurred between 1967 and 1979, during which period the number of committee and personal staff employees grew from 7,014 to 13,276.[3] This sharp increase was due, in large part, to the hostility that characterized the relationship between Congress and President Richard Nixon—it reflected the legislators' desire to put their institution on a more equal footing with the White House in terms of information and expertise. By 2006, the number of congressional staff had reached approximately 15,150.

The week after Thanksgiving 2004 was occupied with more schooling, this time at Harvard University's "Program for Newly Elected Members of Congress." The John F. Kennedy School of Government sponsored this bipartisan policy-oriented program, bringing to campus an impressive array of academics and policy experts to lead seminars on issues that were likely to be on the agenda during the upcoming congressional session. Twenty-four of the thirty-nine new members of Congress accepted Harvard's invitation to participate in this program, which tapped into a completely different set of concerns than the administrative discussions that had comprised the Capitol Hill orientation just two weeks earlier.

The thirteen Democrats and eleven Republicans were given another large binder, promising several more days of information overload. The material in the inside pocket of this binder included an invitation to attend a bipartisan conference on health care policy for selected representatives and senators, to be held January 13–15, 2005, in Florida. As a physician, Joe Schwarz naturally was interested in health care issues, but he and Matt both were amused by the notion of going to Florida less than two weeks after Joe's swearing-in. Somehow the tasks of establishing offices on Capitol Hill and in the district, as well as finding housing in Washington, seemed more pressing.

The inside pocket of the binder also contained a calendar for the coming year, provided by the Office of the House Democratic Leader, Nancy Pelosi of California. Few things are as fluid as these congressional calendars; each party's leadership, in both the House and the Senate, routinely put out updated versions of daily, weekly, monthly, and annual calendars. Even a cursory glance at the calendars reflects the concern that members of Congress have for knowing when their chamber will be voting on the measures it is considering. Each day is clearly marked for "votes" or "no votes," which, among other purposes, assists members in planning their travel schedules between Washington and their home states or districts. Joe and Matt realized just how seriously congressmen and -women take the business of travel when they learned that the major airlines make specialists available at dedicated phone numbers to address the travel needs of MCs and their senior staffers.

The first substantive meeting during the Harvard program focused on the federal budget. (This topic prompted more doodling by Congressman-elect Schwarz, whose notes are adorned with several block "M" drawings, much like the logos on the 50-yard line in Michigan Stadium and at center court in Crisler Arena, where the Wolverines play basketball. This time the artwork was particularly elegant—influenced, perhaps, by the Ivy League surroundings—and colored in with yellow highlighter reminiscent of the University of Michigan's signature "maize and blue" colors.) The federal budget survey was followed by a discussion of "The Politics of Appropriations and Budget." After that, the program continued with seminars on "Public and Family Responsibilities," "Making an Impact as a New Member," and "Nuclear Terrorism." The meetings—conducted by people who had served in Congress or who had worked closely with the policy issues under discussion—moved along through the next couple of days, covering population problems, issues related to globalization, changes in American families, Congress and the media, and America's youth. There was also a tour of the John F. Kennedy Library, followed by a dinner on the library grounds.

During this six-week period, there was no such thing as "spare time." Both Joe and Matt wanted to put together teams of staff members for Washington as well as the district offices as soon as possible. While the pace was hectic, they were, as Matt put it "having a lot more fun than anything that losing the primary or the general [election] could have resulted in."

Having taken on the title of chief of staff, Matt envisioned the near future as one in which he would travel frequently between Washington and Michigan. His most immediate task was to hire someone to supervise the Washington-based staff—someone with Capitol Hill experience and a thorough understanding of the congressional system and the policymaking process. Matt interviewed four people for the job, and then had Joe meet with each of them. Eventually, they chose Chuck Yessaian, who, in his mid-twenties, was the youngest of the job candidates but the only one with any ties to the state of Michigan. Given the title of legislative director, he would undertake, among other duties, supervision of the battery of soon-to-be-named legislative assistants in Congressman Schwarz's Capitol Hill office.

Yessaian had grown up in Northville, a suburban community situated between Detroit and Ann Arbor. A baseball scholarship took him to Lewis University in Romeoville, Illinois. After graduating with a history major in January 2000, Chuck returned to Michigan and first became involved in politics while working on the unsuccessful reelection campaign of Senator Spencer Abraham that year. Though disappointed that his candidate had been defeated—unexpectedly—by Democratic House member Debbie Stabenow, Chuck was still enthusiastic about politics. Like many college graduates who simply head off to Washington in search of government-related work, Chuck had moved to D.C. in January 2001 without any solid job prospects. He worked for a brief time with the government affairs division of the Armenian National Committee and then interviewed for an entry-level position on the staff of the House Transportation and Infrastructure Committee, where he quickly learned that, from the perspective of his colleagues on Capitol Hill, he had no political experience. Sure, he had done some campaign work and had had a brief stint as a lobbyist, but, as Chuck explained, to "the Hill people, everything you do outside the Hill means nothing."

Chuck described his early position on the committee staff as "the lowest staff assistant imaginable. I answered phones and moved furniture. ... I was really a glorified furniture mover, which was fine. I was good at it, and had done a lot of it in college." He had begun working for the committee on September 6, 2001, leading Chuck to claim with a grin, "Yeah, I had five days of sanity before the 9/11 attacks." Between the terrorist attacks and the subsequent anthrax mail scares, as well as a series of particularly frightening sniper attacks in the Washington, D.C., area, he explains, "a lot of people were scared out of D.C., creating even greater job movement than usual." Chuck soon began doing more substantive work for the Oversight Subcommittee of Transportation and Infrastructure, and, in late winter of 2003, he interviewed for a position as legislative assistant (LA) in the office of Fred Upton (R-Mich.). His committee staff experience and his background as a Michigan native were attractive to the Upton office. This new job was a move up the Hill hierarchy, exposing him to a wider range of issues. After being on the Hill for just a little over three years, then, Chuck was ready in late 2004 to make the jump to legislative director in the Schwarz office—an impressive accomplishment, to be sure—but also a reflection of the considerable fluctuation in congressional staff positions.

In his new position, Yessaian inherited three newly appointed legislative assistants. Two had been active in the Schwarz campaign and had been invited to remain on the congressman's staff. Mark Ratner (whose perceptions of the campaign were noted in chapter 2) had worked for Joe during his days in the Michigan state senate and then had served briefly as a substitute teacher before rejoining Schwarz on the campaign trail. Louie Meizlish was a recent graduate of the University of Michigan and a veteran of the campaign as well. Following Joe Schwarz's victory, Louie decided to defer his admission to law school at Wayne State University in Detroit in order to experience life on the Hill. Meghan Kolassa, a thirty-one-year-old attorney and a life-long friend of Joe's daughter Brennan, had worked for Schwarz when he was in the state senate, and she was now invited to join his Washington staff. In addition to these three, Chuck expected to hire one or two more LAs.

A fourth hire was Rob Blackwell, who was given the title of staff assistant. Rob had first met Dr. Joe Schwarz as a frightened youngster whose tonsils needed to be removed. Afterward, the two stayed in touch, and after working on the congressional campaign, Rob was invited to join the staff in Washington. His job description included, as Chuck put it, "everything from helping out with the schedule, to being Joe's bodyman,* to playing gatekeeper in the front office." Rob, Louie, and Mark, who knew each other from their days on the campaign trail, agreed to share an apartment in Washington.

January 3, 2005, was an unseasonably warm Monday in D.C. The skies were overcast and the thermometer reached a humid 60 degrees—weather more befitting St. Patrick's Day than the first work day after the New Year's holiday. Capitol Hill was busy, as many congressmen were settling into new offices, and those newly elected were settling into a whole new life. The hallways of the House office buildings (Cannon, Rayburn, and Longworth—all named for former Speakers) echoed with the sounds of furniture being moved and of people calling out to one another. The hallway outside Room 128 Cannon was no exception.

The area designated for staff in the Schwarz office was in a state of chaos. A small round conference table stood at the front of the room, and an aisle separated two rows of desks that were partitioned off by file

---

*A *bodyman* is the person who shuttles the elected official from place to place; holds the coat, briefcase, or suitcase; and knows when to have a container of coffee, as opposed to bottled water or soda on hand.

cabinets. Someday, either an LA or an intern would sit at each desk; the room would be organized and the staff would be productive. On this first day of business in 2005, however, organization and productivity seemed a long way off.

Chuck Yessaian conducted the first meeting of his new staff at mid-morning. Meeting the supervisor is always awkward, particularly when the person in charge and the staff are contemporaries in terms of age. Moreover, since this group of staff members already knew each other, but not him, Chuck wanted to strike the right balance between approachability and taking charge. He began by impressing upon the staff that it was incumbent on them to know, to the best of their ability, where the voters in the district, the moderates and the Mainstreeters, the Republican delegation from Michigan, and the House party leadership stood on every issue. "The boss is going to ask us those questions, and saying to him, 'I'll get back to you, Congressman,' is not an acceptable answer." Chuck also told them that the office would need at least three days to reply to a request for Congressman Schwarz to cosponsor or sign on to a piece of legislation, but that such requests coming from other members of Congress would take priority in his daily conversations with Joe. Chuck warned, "Other members will try to bully you because you are new. Be polite but do not let that happen. We need some time to figure out who the congressman likes, and who he doesn't."

Yessaian went on to delineate some very basic facts of congressional life. He explained that the legislative assistants would be divided up by issue area and that he intended to spend the rest of the week interviewing applicants for the one or two LA positions that were to be added to the staff. Then he listed hard-and-fast office rules, which, he said were in no particular order:

- Nobody speaks to the press.
- The congressman's schedule is not to be known outside of our office.
- The congressman wants to see as many constituents as possible if they are visiting the office.

- Standard business attire—suits for the men and office-appropriate dress for the women—is to be worn when Congress is in session. Khaki slacks and polo shirts can be worn when Congress is not in session and there is virtually no chance of any surprise meetings taking place. No jeans.
- Call the House Clerk when you are not sure what is going on. That office can tell you what bill is on the floor, what time sessions are scheduled to begin and end, and so on.
- Our office will open at 9:00 a.m. every day and will stay open until 5:30 or 6:30 p.m. when Congress is in session. When Congress is not in session, the office will close between 5:00 and 5:30 p.m.
- Make sure that this office knows where you are and that you always have your cell phone and BlackBerry with you.
- Don't freak out when the alarms go off and we are evacuated. It's not infrequent in the post–9/11 world.
- Learn the rules of the House.
- Know how to cover for each other.

Chuck ended the discussion about office rules and decorum with the clincher, "At the end of the day, it's all about constituents."

The tone of the meeting grew less formal and more like a college bull session when Chuck began talking about reputation. He advised that offices do earn reputations in the aggregate, and that the staff of the previous member representing Michigan's Seventh District had not enjoyed a very positive reputation. He urged his new charges to go to after-hours receptions, learn their way around the Hill, and get to know other staffs. "We want to be known as helpful to others on the Hill," Chuck encouraged, "and hard-working."

Finally, Chuck got down to brass tacks. "Getting the mail out is the part of the job that sucks," he stated bluntly, and everyone laughed. Two weeks was the expected turn-around time for responding to mail. "Make sure your friends and family send personal mail to you at your home address," Chuck instructed. "All mail coming to the Hill gets x-rayed off-site, which builds in a considerable delay that the sender is unaware of. You don't want cookies from your Mom to get stale, and you don't want a constituent to think that he or she is being ignored."

Chuck had one more bit of information to share before returning to his office: the Schwarz operation expected to learn of the congressman's committee assignments the next day, and that would have an impact on how the policy issues were divided among the staff members. With that, the first staff meeting was over, and everyone went back to the tasks of setting up their spaces in the staff room and waiting for the technology folks to come in to hook up their computers. As a group, Mark, Louie, Meegan, and Rob walked upstairs to the second floor of the Cannon Building to be photographed for their credentials and the ID cards they would wear, either clipped to a belt or lapel, or on a chain around the neck. As they went on that group outing, they looked excited and a little anxious—a young congressional staff with a lot to learn.

During the day, other members of the congressional campaign team, as well as friends and family, arrived in Washington to be part of the swearing-in festivities. Some of the campaign staff would return to Michigan to take on positions in the district offices, but January 3rd and 4th were days to celebrate. There was no shortage of parties and receptions at which they could all be together again to savor the victory, but an almost imperceptible difference was in the air. Representative Schwarz was no longer Joe or Dr. Schwarz to the young staffers with whom he had shared the rigors of the campaign trail. Now, in a different town, with a different atmosphere, and with a different set of rules, Joe was "the congressman." While they had once worked together for a common electoral prize, they were now separate: a member of the United States Congress and his staff. Schwarz still had the same smile, the same warm greeting for each of these young people who had seen him through a tough primary and the subsequent general election, but there was no getting around it— the situation had changed.

On the night of January 3, Washington was abuzz with private parties and receptions in honor of the swearing-in of the 109th Congress. One such gathering was hosted by Blue Cross and Blue Shield of Michigan, CMS Energy, Dykema Gossett PLLC, the Kellogg Company, and the University of Michigan Health System. Held in the Sky Room and Sky Terrace

Rep. Schwarz on the steps of the Capitol. Joe quickly organized his staff on the Hill, and while he was still the same person many of them had worked with over the campaign, things were different now—they were in D.C., and "Joe" was now "the congressman."

atop the Hotel Washington at 15th and Pennsylvania Avenue, this invitation-only affair featured Congressman-elect Joe Schwarz as the honored guest. There was a slight mist in the air, and Washington after dark twinkled below as the Schwarz team enjoyed drinks and hors d'oeuvres, and the taste of victory. For just a few hours, Battle Creek and the Seventh District seemed far away. This night was about celebration, as most of the next day would be. But everyone knew that the jubilation would last another twenty-four hours at most; then, friends and family would head for home, and Congressman Schwarz and his staff would get to work.

It was still warm outside on Swearing-In Day, January 4, 2005, and there was intermittent rain in the morning. Inside, the Cannon Building swarmed with people. Most of the offices were hosting small private receptions of coffee, pastries, and fruit—it was a particularly busy morning for the Capitol Hill catering service. Friends, family, staff, and other interested people stopped by Room 128 to visit with the new

Congressman Schwarz and, once more, wish him well. House colleagues from Michigan, Republicans Fred Upton and Mike Rogers, stopped to say hello and to welcome Joe into the fold. There were also a number of press people milling about, looking to write stories about the oldest member of the freshman class. Celebrated journalist David Broder of the *Washington Post* stopped by to meet with Joe and to interview some of the congressman's friends. Widely known as "the dean of the Washington press corps," Broder already had some ties to Schwarz. They had met some years ago on Beaver Island in northern Michigan, where Broder has a summer home next door to good friends of Dr. Schwarz. But Broder had gotten to know him better during the presidential primaries in 2000, when Joe was heading up the McCain campaign in Michigan and Broder was reporting on McCain's candidacy.

Joe left his reception for a short while to walk over with one of his young staffers to the Office of the Speaker of the House, where he was to pick up his membership credentials. On the way, he compared his feelings on this first day in Congress to how he had felt on the first day he practiced medicine: "The first night that I was really doing medicine, I was a surgical resident. When I first heard somebody say 'Dr. Schwarz,' I looked over my shoulder to see who they were speaking to. At the very beginning," he continued with a chuckle, "I was frightened. When patients started to go sour on me...I could have filled my pants." The beginnings of his medical career and of his congressional career, Joe noted, were similar only in that each represented the undertaking of an entirely new set of responsibilities. Today, there was not any of the fear or anxiety that he had felt that first night in the surgical ward—in part, Joe reflected, because a person in his twenties is more likely to get rattled than one in his sixties.

Schwarz also mentioned that during these past few days he had been having a lot of fun. The day before, for example, while his staff had been putting the office together, he and his daughter Brennan had attended an event for new members of Congress at the White House, where they had had their picture taken with the president and First Lady. "You really have to enjoy those kinds of special moments. So far, I'm having a great time," Joe said, before quickly acknowledging that the work was soon to replace the fun.

When Joe arrived at the lobby outside the Speaker's office, he was directed to a table covered with packets for the members whose last names began with letters in the latter half of the alphabet, where he was handed a large brown envelope. After signing for his credentials, he recognized Tom Osborne, a Republican congressman from Nebraska, and greeted him with a friendly "Hi, Coach, good to see you." Osborne, who was picking up his credentials for his third term in Congress, was probably more widely known for his twenty-five years as head coach of the University of Nebraska Cornhuskers football team. "Nice to see you, too," Osborne said with a smile and a warm handshake. There was a spirit of camaraderie in the air as members came and went and moved through the crowded halls that morning.

The brown envelope given to each member of the House contained a membership pin, a vote ID card, an auto license plate, and a set of evacuation and emergency instructions. Members of Congress are provided secure cover in case of a national emergency, and these instructions outlined the procedures and directions to be followed if the situation were to call for it. Before September 11, 2001, members rarely paid much attention to these instructions, but now they are more likely to glance over this material, or at least have a staff member brief them on it.

The vote ID is a white plastic card, the size of a credit card. It fits into one of the forty voting machine stations located on the chair backs of the seats situated along the aisles in the House chamber. The cards are personalized electronically, and the vote machines are card readers that offer three vote choices. When activated, the machine indicates the member's vote by the color of the light that is illuminated next to the member's name on an electronic "scoreboard" located on the wall above the press gallery: green for "yes;" red for "no;" and amber for "present." This electronic voting system was implemented in the House of Representatives in 1973 to minimize the number of lengthy roll call votes.

The cardboard "license plate" can be placed on the dashboard of any car in which a congressman is riding. In the past, members were issued traditional metal plates identifying a car as belonging to a member of Congress, but both security concerns and convenience make the cardboard plates more sensible. Congressman Schwarz had not brought his own car with him to Washington, D.C., so his plate would be kept in Rob Blackwell's car. Rob, as bodyman, had been assigned the task of picking Joe up each morning and driving him to the office, as well as taking the congressman to various meetings and appointments off the Hill.

The membership pin that Joe found in his brown envelope is typically worn on a lapel or collar to identify a current member of the House. The design changes with every Congress; the pin for the 109th Congress displayed the House's eagle symbol surrounded by a blue border. In the previous Congress, the House pin had featured a gaudier red, white, and blue background, leading staffers to joke about whether the pin had been designed by a clown. A number engraved on the back of each pin approximates seniority, but, more importantly, it is used for record-keeping by the Office of the Sergeant at Arms. Looking at the back of his pin, Joe mused, "Hmm…434 out of 435. Shows you about how much I rate around here."

On the walk back to his office, Joe encountered the Democratic Party leader in the House, Nancy Pelosi. He introduced himself and said good morning, and she greeted him graciously and wished him well. After that short exchange, Joe said with self-deprecating humor, "I'm sure she's saying to herself, 'Who is that schmuck and why is he saying hello to me?'"

The coffee receptions were winding down as Joe returned to the Cannon Building. People were getting ready to go to the Swearing-In or to one of the many swearing-in parties that were already underway. The hallway outside Joe's office was still crowded, however, since the office immediately next door housed another freshman who was surrounded by a considerable throng of well-wishers. Luis Fortuño was the newly elected representative from Puerto Rico, the first Republican to be elected from that territory. Like the District of Columbia and the territories of American Samoa, Guam, and the U.S. Virgin Islands, Puerto Rico has a nonvoting member in the House. Between those joining the Schwarz group and those celebrating with Fortuño, the hallway was virtually impassable, and it took some time for folks to navigate their way to the Capitol building.

Members are limited in the number of guests they can have in the House gallery for the official Swearing-In and the session's first reading of the roll. Joe's daughter Brennan, his brother Frank, and his sister Janet sat together for the ceremony. Frank's sons, Robert and Fred, who were both in their late forties, sat in another section of the gallery seats to watch their uncle take his oath of office. Brennan was proud of her dad, and happy for him, knowing how important this day was. As a young girl she had often felt embarrassed to be in the public spotlight as the daughter of the mayor. That, however, had been years ago, and this Swearing-In Day on Capitol Hill was, she said, "very cool." Janet, too, felt a great deal of pride in her younger brother's accomplishment and was certainly proud of him on this day. She found herself wishing that their parents were still alive and able "to share such a momentous family occasion."

Friends and supporters of the new congressman watched the ceremony on television at a lovely reception paid for by the Schwarz campaign fund, though it was being held in the E Street offices of R.B. Murphy and Associates, a Washington lobbying firm. The setting was a beautiful old brownstone in a very desirable section of D.C., befitting the good food, drink, and laughter that were in abundance on that January afternoon. A loud cheer of approval could be heard on the street outside the elegant building when Congressman Schwarz answered the roll call for the first time.

A much smaller group of Schwarz intimates enjoyed a late afternoon happy hour at the Old Ebbitt Grill. Located near the White House, the restaurant opened in 1856 and became a favorite of presidents Grant, Cleveland, Harding, and Theodore Roosevelt. A Washington institution, the Ebbitt is a place for political people to see and to be seen. The happy hour mood was festive, though a bit of weariness was setting in. People were beginning to think about going home, and the Schwarz staffers were looking ahead to their new challenges.

Later that evening, an even smaller, low-key gathering took place at another Washington landmark restaurant, The Caucus Room. In a private dining room, Joe and his staff, family, and close friends had an opportunity to visit and reflect. This group took a more personal satisfaction in Joe's success. The congressman spoke, singling out several people. He thanked his friend Don Black, with whom he had served in Vietnam. Remarking that the only negative thing he could say about Captain Black was that he was an Ohio State Buckeye, Joe smiled and told his guests that the two of them tried to go to the Michigan–Ohio State game together every year. Then, becoming a little wistful, Joe noted that Don had once saved his life. At one location during the war, when he thought that Joe's quarters were unacceptable, Don had insisted that Joe to move to his own nicer and more spacious arrangement. Shortly thereafter, Joe's former quarters were leveled by a bomb. "Thanks again, Don," the congressman finished, "and thanks for being here."

Joe also recognized his brother and sister, and he swelled with pride when he introduced his daughter. Tears welled in his eyes at the mention of his late wife, Anne, as he honored her memory and wished that she were with him. Joe thanked a few others by name, and jokingly introduced a college professor who was standing in a corner, either taking notes or talking into his "damned tape recorder...he actually thinks what we are doing here is worth writing about."

The evening wound down, good-byes were exchanged, and the congressman went to his hotel for some much-needed rest. Tomorrow the work would begin.

4

Learning the Ropes

In the movie *The Distinguished Gentleman*, Eddie Murphy plays a con-man turned congressman and so revisits many of the themes addressed in the Frank Capra classic, *Mr. Smith Goes to Washington*. At one point in the story, Murphy's character is standing before a group of touring schoolchildren, struggling to answer a question posed by one of the kids, when suddenly a colleague calls out, "Hey, Congressman, we have to get to the floor for a vote—don't you hear those bells ringing?" Murphy's response, "Oh, I've been wondering what those bells mean," is certainly comic, but it is also rather profound, for it implies that an MC has much to learn in order to do the job.

Among the many immediate topics to which a new member of Congress must attend are the complexities of the committee system, the role of caucuses and work groups, and the discovery of like-minded colleagues, while struggling, meanwhile, with the problems of securing personal housing in the D.C. area and somehow keeping in touch with constituents in the home district. In the early days of his term, Joe Schwarz had to determine which committee assignments to seek, which caucuses to join, and whom to pay attention to and whom to ignore. He had to find a place to live, and he had to find ways to stay attentive to the folks back home. In a sense, it was yet another orientation exercise in learning the ropes of the congressional mechanism.

The committee system is absolutely central to the policymaking process. Congress handles roughly 10,000 bills in any given two-year cycle; this enormous workload must be divided in some manageable way. Standing committees—permanent panels that are set up around specific policy areas—provide the structure for handling the volume of bills introduced, and they are essential to a House member's life on the Hill. It is through service on standing committees that individual members can develop expertise, interact with fellow MCs, and leave a mark on public policy that they hope will serve the public in general and their "back home constituency" in particular.

As Roger Davidson and Walter Oleszek point out, "committees serve two broad purposes: individual and institutional."[1] For the institution, standing committees and their subcommittees are at the heart of policy-making, and it is not often that a bill makes it to the floor of the House or Senate without going through the committee process. For the individual, the committees to which a congressman or -woman is assigned will help to shape his or her career. Members typically seek assignments to committees that consider legislation important to their particular districts.

Committee assignments are made by each party in the chamber, and the leadership exerts a great deal of influence in the process. The total number of Democrats and Republicans on any standing committee reflects the strength of each party in the chamber. If a party controls 55 percent of the seats in the House, for example, it receives 55 percent of the seats on each standing committee. In any given Congress, there are about twenty standing committees in the House, varying in size from a low of just under a dozen members to a high of seventy to eighty members.

The work of each standing committee is further divided among a number of subcommittees that are comprised of members of the standing committee who develop particular expertise in the specific subject matters or policy areas that define the subcommittees' jurisdictions. Members of Congress take their committee work very seriously, forging relationships with colleagues that are fostered by common policy interests and the dynamics of a small-group work situation.

After the victory in the 2004 primary, Joe Schwarz and Matt Marsden began discussing the committee assignments that would be commensurate with Joe's interests and ability to benefit the Seventh District. In a lunch conversation in August, they quickly agreed that an assignment to the Committee on Education and the Workforce would be great. Joe believed deeply in the importance of education and was interested in all levels of the educational process; because of his medical training, he had a particular appreciation for science education, as well as a much broader interest in science generally. Consequently, Joe and Matt determined that a seat on the Science Committee was also attractive.

Several other committees would allow Congressman Schwarz to directly serve constituent needs. Because farming is a major industry in Michigan's Seventh District, and because the retiring congressman, Nick Smith, had served on the Agriculture Committee, a seat on Agriculture would be welcomed. The Transportation and Infrastructure Committee also seemed an attractive possibility, in part because Interstate 94, which runs east-to-west through the district, is badly in need of repair and widening in some places. Moreover, a seat on Transportation might enable Joe to be helpful to Amtrak, which his own commitment to rail travel and his enjoyable experience on the campaign train trip both inclined him to favor.

Finally, there was the matter of defense. For a number of reasons, an assignment to the Armed Services Committee would be desirable. First, the Hart-Dole-Inouye Federal Center in Battle Creek is a huge Department of Defense operation that employs numerous constituents, and it had to be protected in a time of budget shortages and military reorganization. There is also a National Guard base in the Seventh District, and base relocations were looming in the near future. Joe's intelligence experience in the CIA and his service in Vietnam might appear, at first blush, to have made him a natural for an appointment to Armed Services. His freshman status, however, worked against him, since, typically, freshmen are not assigned to that powerful committee. Moreover, because of the many hot spots in the world, as well as the ongoing war on terror, the Armed Services Committee was likely to remain front and center in the news for the immediate future, which would make membership on that committee even more desirable for seasoned, ambitious congressmen and congresswomen.

New Republican House members request their committee assignments by submitting a letter indicating their preferences to the party's

Steering Committee, which, because the Republicans held the majority in the 109th Congress, was controlled by the Speaker of the House. (The Democratic Party leadership in the House plays a similar role in determining the committee assignments of new House Democrats.) There is no guarantee that the new members' preferences will be honored, and most new members arrive with relatively limited expectations regarding the assignments they will be given. However deeply they may care about their own priorities and those of their constituents, the reality is that freshmen are going to do what the leadership tells them to do when it comes to committee assignments.

Congressman-elect Schwarz requested assignments to any combination of the following committees: Agriculture, Armed Services, Education and the Workforce, and Transportation and Infrastructure. On his visits to Washington between the election and the Swearing-In, he met with as many members of the Steering Committee as possible. More than simply courtesy calls made by a new House member, these meetings actually gave Joe a chance to introduce himself and talk about his interests and abilities, and, ultimately, to reinforce in person the committee requests he had made in writing.

Meanwhile, experienced members of the new congressman's staff also spoke to their counterparts on the staffs of Steering Committee members in order to make the case for a particular assignment for their boss. Chuck Yessaian, Joe's legislative director, bluntly described the process: "Staff members lobby like crazy on behalf of their congressmen, and are sometimes relentless in doing so." The urgency of these efforts derives from the realization that committee assignments do, in large part, drive and define an MC's substantive policy life, and that the assignment process is also the very first important interaction that a new member has with his or her party leadership. Consequently, the entire Schwarz office took the committee assignment process very seriously.

Congressman Schwarz and his staff were pleased when Joe's committee assignments—Agriculture, Science, and Armed Services—were delivered by letter from the Office of the Speaker of the House. Each committee fit Joe's principal interest areas, and he was particularly thrilled with the Armed Services appointment. Chuck remembers his own reaction as "pleasantly shocked." The staff subsequently learned that Joe had probably not been assigned to Transportation and Infrastructure because two of his colleagues in the Michigan Republican delegation, Peter Hoekstra and Vernon Ehlers, already sat on that committee. It was also likely that Joe's moderate leanings, compared with the more conservative opposition to teachers unions that characterized the views of most of the Republicans on the Committee on Education and the Workforce, had played a role in keeping him off that committee. The Science Committee was, however, a fine substitute, since there is considerable overlap in the committees' jurisdictions as well as in the policy areas they deal with.

Even as Congressman Schwarz was beginning to feel a part of the legislative scene professionally, he had a number of personal issues to sort out. One was travel between Washington and the home district, to which he wanted to return every week, so as not to lose touch with his constituents. He also hoped to continue seeing patients, and he planned to be at his medical office in Battle Creek on three or four Monday mornings each month. Throughout his first year, Schwarz did continue to see patients, and he traveled home as close to once a week as he could manage.

Another significant issue was housing. He had done some initial looking during a November trip to Washington, when a realtor took him to see several apartments. Michigan Congresswoman Candice Miller had advised him not to live on Capitol Hill. She had done so her first year in Congress, she told Joe, and had found it impossible to feel that she was ever away from work. Congressional life was consuming enough, she observed, and getting away from the Hill to unwind was important. Miller had moved to nearby suburban Virginia, but she had a car in town—a complication that Joe hoped to avoid. While he didn't necessarily want to live on Capitol Hill, he had hoped to find a place in the District.

Apartments are scarce in Washington, and they are expensive. The new congressman certainly wanted to bring some routine into his life, which is difficult when living out of a suitcase in a hotel. As he surveyed the available apartments, however, he became dispirited.

> I looked at a number of places, but they were all basements. They call them "English basements," probably as a way to make them sound like something other than basements. Call them whatever you want...to me it's a friggin' basement. They were all a little musty, and the cockroaches I saw had to be on steroids. I kept thinking to myself, "I really don't want this." So, to make a little conversation, I say to this lady who's showing me around, "Do they flood, these basement apartments?" This question elicited a pregnant pause, and she finally says, "Almost never." I had to laugh at that.

Joe stayed on at the Hyatt Hotel on New Jersey Avenue, which he claimed had a "pretty fair rate" for members of Congress—"at least for Washington, D.C. prices"—while he continued to search for an apartment. As the weeks rolled by, some of his freshmen colleagues asked, "What's the difference if it's a basement? It's only three or four days a week." But Joe dug in his heels. "I just didn't want to live in a basement, so I let the search for a place drag on for a bit."

One day, he saw an apartment in a building on Pennsylvania Avenue, between the White House and the Capitol. "I had actually been in the building earlier," Joe said, "but they were showing me some two bedroom apartments, which cost your arm, your leg, your firstborn, and everything you have in your bank account." But this time, he was shown a small, one-bedroom; light and airy, it had "a little open air porch that you could use nine months out of the year here—particularly if you are accustomed to Michigan winters." It was neat and furnished, and not far from the Cannon Building. Joe's offer was accepted, and then,

> ...they wouldn't take my personal check. They knew I was a member of Congress, and a physician...and they wouldn't take my check. I said, "Look, I'll give you the name of my banker in Battle Creek if you want." They said "No! We want a cashiers check or bank draft. We will not take your personal check." I thought to myself, "Well, screw you," and walked away from the deal. I hadn't been through this kind of nonsense in years. The whole episode was like trying to find an apartment when you're in college.

Joe's decision to stand on principle cost him another week or so, but then another unit (similar to the one he had walked away from) in the same building became available. The owner of this apartment took his check, and he moved some of his things from Michigan to Washington. By early March, the congressman was out of the Hyatt and settled in his apartment.

Early in his term, Schwarz began to build relationships with different actors in the political system. Members of Congress are, of course, presented with numerous points of view, and they must quickly decide whom to listen to, whom to seek out for information, and frankly, whom to ignore.

In his seminal study of congressional behavior—which, more than thirty years after publication, remains instructive for understanding the universe in which members of Congress work—John Kingdon identifies a number of cues to which legislators respond. These cues include the members' constituencies, fellow congressmen, party leadership and committee leadership, interest groups, the executive branch (the president and his administration), staff, and the media.[2] Simply stated, Kingdon's conclusion is that members must weigh how their decision making will be viewed by the varied populations with whom they must interact.

A month after taking office—even before he had found a place to live—Joe was able to see how contentious his universe could be. On February 2, 2005, in his annual State of the Union address, President Bush pushed vigorously for reform of the Social Security program. Bush's plan would allow American workers to invest a portion of their Social Security taxes in stocks or bonds rather than having all of those funds go into the traditional program that had been established in 1935, during the administration of Franklin D. Roosevelt. While very popular with many conservatives, the president's proposal proved quite divisive within his own Republican Party in Congress. (Not surprisingly, it enjoyed little support from congressional Democrats).

Congressman Schwarz was not enthusiastic about the president's plan. "I want to see a specific proposal," he said. "The specifics and the numbers. I am someone who would be, looking at quantifying reform, a minimalist. Do enough to make sure that the system is sound, but the system has worked so well for so long, I don't think it needs any wholesale change."[3] With that statement, Schwarz placed himself in the middle of a well-publicized battle over the Bush plan to revamp Social Security.

In response to the growing controversy, a conservative political advocacy group known as the Club for Growth bought television time in three areas of the country, targeting Republican legislators from those areas for their unwillingness to support the plan. It came as no great surprise that interest groups would enter the fray at this point, but it was a bit striking that a freshman member of Congress, just one month into his term, would be targeted. The other Republicans attacked in the Club for Growth television ad were Lincoln Chafee, who had represented Rhode Island in the U.S. Senate since 1999, and Sherwood Boehlert, a twelve-term member of the House from New York.

"This ad is a gentle message about the virtues of personal accounts and a blunt message that we are watching their actions on this issue with great interest," the president of the Club for Growth said of the ad campaign. For his part, Schwarz was dismissive, claiming, "I am always kind of quasi-amused at this 'ready, fire, aim,' approach."[4] In fact, the Club for Growth had been very active in its support of Joe's primary opponent, Brad Smith, so no one in the Schwarz operation was really shocked by this latest assault. Less philosophical than the congressman, however, Matt Marsden called the ad "ridiculous." And in reaction to the menacing statement that the right-wing organization was watching the congressman's actions with "great interest," Matt retorted, "That's fine. They watched us through the whole election last year, and they watched us win."[5]

There was a lesson in this early sparring, and the Schwarz office knew what it was. Some organized interests do not want you in Congress, so it's important to counter that threat by developing networks of people and groups who do want you there. To that end, Joe joined a number of caucuses and began to look for like-minded legislators with whom he could work. For its part, the Club for Growth made good on its promise to watch Schwarz carefully—it would play a very active role in the 2006 campaign for the seat from Michigan's Seventh District.

Caucuses, which are usually bipartisan and centered around specific public policy areas, are informal groupings of House members (and

This frame is taken from a television ad that the Club for Growth ran in the Seventh District shortly after Joe assumed office. The attack on Schwarz as a "liberal" in disguise presaged the strategy that the Club for Growth would pursue throughout the 2006 election cycle.

occasionally senators). There are numerous caucuses to choose from, allowing those who join to keep tabs on particular issues they care about and enabling interested parties outside of Congress to know which legislators are engaged in which policies. Thus, membership in a caucus not only says something about the legislator, but also sends a signal to lobbyists, the media, and other relevant actors that the caucus member is approachable on a particular topic.

Congressman Schwarz joined nearly three dozen caucuses covering a wide range of subjects. He became a member of the Northern Border Caucus, the Automotive Caucus, and the Passenger Rail Caucus—all directly related to the politics of Michigan. He also sat in six different health caucuses and nine caucuses focused in some way on foreign policy and international relations. Joe paid particular attention to the China Caucus and the World Health Caucus, since Asian affairs and health issues were of great concern to him. For some congressmen and -women, membership in a caucus is little more than a statement of interest in a subject area, while others are more active in the meetings and discussions that a caucus may sponsor. For freshmen legislators, caucus memberships allow a quick and easy introduction to members of both parties who have similar policy interests and concerns.

Beyond these issue-specific caucuses, another of Joe's memberships played a significant role in his Hill life and in his ability to work with like-minded colleagues. The Tuesday Group, once referred to as a "casual caucus of pragmatic Republicans," now works closely with the Main Street Partnership, which, as noted in chapter 2, gives voice to moderate congressional Republicans. The Tuesday Group became more active in the 109th Congress than it had been in the past, meeting almost every week that Congress was in session—though, ironically, on Wednesday. The group originally intended to meet on the second day of the week, but the weekly congressional calendar now typically runs from Tuesday through Thursday, reserving Monday and Friday for travel. As a result, Wednesday became the second "work day" of most weeks, and, as Washington logic would have it, the Tuesday Group meets on Wednesday.

The standing committee system and the specialized subcommittees that serve each standing committee also provide a built-in peer group for any new member of Congress. It does not take long for a freshman representative to take the measure of his or her committee and subcommittee colleagues, determining who shares similar values and ideologies. Joe was assigned to six subcommittees: the Subcommittee on Strategic Forces and the Subcommittee on Readiness (Armed Services Committee); the Specialty Crops and Foreign Agriculture Programs Subcommittee and the Conservation, Credit, Rural Development and Research Subcommittee (Agriculture Committee); and the Energy Subcommittee and the Environment, Technology, and Standards Subcommittee (Science Committee). Soon he was able to make some early judgments about colleagues on these committees and subcommittees with whom he could share views and information.

It is difficult to overestimate the importance of these associations with other members of Congress. In discussing the various factors that affect how members of Congress decide to vote on any given issue, Kingdon notes that "fellow congressmen appear to be the most important influence on voting decisions."[6] As the more than 5,000 bills introduced every year, and the thousands of amendments attached to those bills, work their way through the legislative process, it stands to reason that members often must rely on like-minded colleagues for information and voting cues. Congressman Schwarz was no exception. "Colleagues have certainly been helpful," Joe observed. "Frankly, I don't think anyone can function effectively here if they don't share ideas and expertise with other members, both Republican and Democrat." Among the group of colleagues whose opinions he valued on a variety of issues, however, one stood out: "I am particularly fortunate for a freshman because of my friendship with Senator McCain. He is so well versed and plugged in. . . . I do not hesitate to pick up the phone and call him to get his take on something or bounce an idea off of him."

The importance of these committee-based and issue-related professional networks was reflected in the invitations extended to Congressman Schwarz soon after he was sworn in. Senator McCain, a senior member of the Senate Armed Services Committee, and Congressman Duncan Hunter (R-Calif.), the chair of the House Committee on Armed Services, asked Joe to join a ten-person congressional delegation to Europe. During the second week in February 2005, the delegation stopped in Ukraine before going to Germany to attend a conference on security. Six weeks later, Schwarz was asked to travel to Iraq with another delegation, also led by Senator McCain, which met with Iraqi leaders, military personnel, and troops. Four governors also made the trip, as did senators Russell Feingold (D-Wisc.) and John Thune (R-S.D.), and House members Mark Kirk (R-Ill.) and Tom Udall (D-N.M.). Congressman Schwarz noted that one of the primary purposes of the trip was to deliver a strong message to Iraqi leaders: "We do hope they understand that the patience of the American people is not endless. We want them to prevail, but this is something that simply has to get moving."

While in Iraq, Schwarz managed to mix in some personal time with the troops. He met with a group of soldiers from Michigan, one of whom (a Michigan State graduate) made a special request of the congressman. "This soldier got a football that he was having signed by the members of Congress," Joe explained. "He wanted me to sign it, and he said to me, 'Even as a University of Michigan graduate, would you write "Go Green" on there?' And I said, 'Absolutely!'" Having served in the armed forces himself and understanding firsthand the demands of military life, Joe felt a special bond with these troops.

As much as he valued his friendship with Senator McCain and respected his expertise on military issues, Joe also found many of the members of the House Armed Service Committee to be helpful and congenial colleagues. "I like, genuinely like and respect, all of my committee chairs," he observed, adding that he had a fine relationship with Duncan Hunter. Two other Republican colleagues on that committee, John Kline of Minnesota and Geoff Davis of Kentucky were especially valuable resources. Both Kline, who had had a twenty-five-year career in the Marine Corps before coming to Congress, and Davis, a graduate of West Point and a former army officer, brought to the work of the committee a knowledge base and perspective that Schwarz prized. Representative Davis was also a member of the Strategic Forces Subcommittee, and he and Joe talked with some frequency and with no small measure of mutual respect.

Congressman Schwarz enjoyed good working relations with several of the Democrats on Armed Services as well. Ike Skelton (D-Mo.), the ranking member on the committee, was described by Schwarz as "a prince of a guy. I enjoy working with him." Joe often looked to Congresswoman Ellen Tauscher (D-Calif.), with whom he sat on the Strategic Forces Subcommittee, for information and cues on nuclear weaponry because he valued her expertise is this area. He was also comfortable sharing information with Mark Udall (D-Colo.), a colleague on the Readiness Subcommittee of Armed Services.

Congressman Schwarz also had praise for and confidence in the staff working for the Armed Services Committee,[7] and he was impressed by the way the work of the committee was conducted. He noted that, beyond the usual committee and subcommittee meetings, Armed Services often sponsored breakfasts at which experts in topics relevant to the committee's jurisdiction would give informal presentations. Schwarz found these sessions informative, and he enjoyed the opportunity to delve into the details of policy.

Representative Schwarz also found colleagues on his other committees with whom he could work easily. He formed a close relationship with the chairman of the Agriculture Committee, Bob Goodlatte (R-Va.), who shared with him a particular interest in veterinary medicine. Goodlatte even came to Joe's district to spend a day with him, meeting people from the farming community in the Michigan Seventh. For a committee chair to spend a day in a freshman's district is no small statement of support

Rep. Bob Goodlatte (R-Va.), chair of the House Agriculture Committee, spent the day with Congressman Schwarz back in Michigan speaking with farm constituents about their concerns. Goodlatte (at left in both photos) was an important colleague for Joe as he learned to master the congressional committee system, while Joe's medical training made him an important source of information on veterinary issues, a valuable asset for the Agriculture chair.

and respect. Joe also had a warm relationship with Tom Osborne (R-Neb.), with whom he shared a subcommittee assignment.

On the Science Committee, Joe worked well with fellow Michigander Vernon Ehlers, chair of the Subcommittee on Environment, Technology, and Standards. "I am very comfortable with Vern," Joe remarked, "in part, I suppose, because we both have technical educations." Ehlers, who was beginning his seventh term in the House as Joe was starting his congressional career, is a physicist with a Ph.D. from the University of California, Berkeley. The two shared a mutual respect for each other's work.

As a freshman, Congressman Schwarz took his committee and subcommittee assignments very seriously, a trait that characterizes active and respected legislators. He worked hard to prepare for meetings and recognized that these committees were his most important substantive work groups. But it was not the congressman alone who looked to other members for cues. Congressional staffers comprise something of a parallel universe to the one in which the MCs operate. Congressman Schwarz's legislative director, Chuck Yessaian, for example, made it a point to know where every member of the Michigan Republican delegation in the House stood on every issue. He gathered this information by checking and sharing notes with his counterparts in the other members' offices. He was also aware of the substantive issue expertise developed by these members. After twenty years in Congress, Fred Upton was well versed on telecommunications policy, for example, while Mike Rogers and Peter Hoekstra were looked to as experts on intelligence issues, an extremely significant topic in the post–9/11 world.

House members typically specialize in particular issue areas, because the volume of policies with which they deal is so great that no one can be an expert on every issue. Each committee has several members who have become specialists in the areas that fall under the committee's jurisdiction, and people on the Hill are aware of these representatives' legislative expertise. Not surprisingly, Chuck reported, "the boss has become the go-to guy in the Michigan Republican delegation that everybody gravitates to on health policy. The fact that he's practiced medicine for more than thirty years, knows what he is talking about, and is a likable guy may have something to do with that." Chuck also communicated with staffers whose "bosses" were not from Michigan, but who shared views similar to Joe's. Mark Kirk (R-Ill.) and Charlie Bass (R-N.H.), both members of the Tuesday Group, were usually good touchstones on most issues. Relying on each other for cues and information is just one of the many coping strategies that new members of Congress must learn, if they are going to be successful.

Of course, colleagues are only one part of the complex set of actors to whom the MC must listen. Another significant actor is the constituency back home. Getting an accurate fix on just what your constituents want you to do, however, is not always easy. Average citizens are not paying much attention to Congress, yet their representatives are always trying to "read" what these constituents want them to do. The Schwarz operation developed a few different techniques to keep abreast of constituent opinion. Like most members of Congress, Joe had staffers back in the district offices clipping relevant items from the many local newspapers published in the district. From articles about issues, letters to the editor, the work of regular columnists, and editorials, the congressman's office can glean a sense of the district's attitude and concerns as portrayed in the print media. Certainly, monitoring the media serves other purposes as well, since, as Kingdon points out, the media itself provides additional cues to which members of Congress respond.

Keeping an eye on the many local newspapers in the district also allows the MC to be a constant figure on the local scene. In addition to issuing regular press releases that often run in these papers without any editing, the representative's office staff studies the local papers for information on local activities and individual accomplishments back home. When a story about a citizen receiving an award from some organization runs in a local paper, efficient congressional staffers know how to quickly get a letter of commendation from the congressman or -woman out to that person. If the office has advance notice, it may even get a letter or proclamation delivered in time to be presented at the award event itself. Often, a master or mistress of ceremonies will announce, "Congressman So-and-So could not be with us today, but asked that his warm congratulations be extended to our award winner." This kind of local presence is invaluable to the MC's reputation, and it is often the result of paying close attention to the most local of media sources.

Another way in which the congressman can keep up with the views of constituents is by tracking public opinion on different issues. As early as the spring of Joe's first year in office, Chief of Staff Matt Marsden put a large white board, covered with a matrix, on the wall of his office. Each column was headed by the name of a county in the district, and each row was labeled with a different issue. At some point, the cells in the matrix would be filled in with poll data indicating the percentage of district residents who found a particular issue most significant to them. Conducting a sound public opinion poll is costly—as Matt put it, "At several thousand dollars a pop, you cannot go buying polls every week." However, the Schwarz team planned to run issue polls two or three times a year to maintain a clear idea of which issues were most important to voters.[8] In early 2005, the poll data indicated that Social Security and health care consistently topped the list of issues that were important to the constituents in the Seventh District. Mindful of that finding, Congressman Schwarz paid close attention to those issues—both in Washington and back home.

A third, very important way in which legislators keep in touch with citizens in the district is to meet with them regularly. Well aware that Washington can be an insular place, Congressman Schwarz did not want to forget that there was life outside the Beltway. In addition to the one-on-one contact he maintained with his patients, he intended to stay in touch by having the district office staffs arrange meetings with groups and constituents, by scheduling open forums with a question-and-answer format, and by accepting invitations to speak to and visit with the many constituents who routinely seek the congressman's ear. Of course, having spent most of his life in Battle Creek, served the city as its mayor, and later risen to president of the Michigan Senate, Joe could also rely some on his own instincts to tell him where the people back home stood on the issues.

The party leadership in Congress serves as another significant cue to members, and so a new legislator must cultivate a relationship with the leaders in his or her chamber. As a member of the majority party in the House, Joe would be in fairly regular contact with the Speaker, the majority leader, and the majority whip. When he was sworn in as a member of the 109th Congress, the Speaker of the House was Dennis Hastert (R-Ill.), whom Joe described as "an amiable fellow and a very good listener." The majority leader was Texan Tom DeLay, a frequent newsmaker and a masterful fund-raiser, who had the reputation of being someone that no one wanted to cross. During Schwarz's term, however, DeLay became embroiled in scandal, resigned his leadership position, and announced that he would not seek reelection to Congress; in February 2006, the Republican Conference elected John Boehner of Ohio to be majority leader. Roy Blunt of Missouri was the majority whip, from which post he tried to remain in constant contact with all Republicans members in order to keep them posted on the schedule of business and upcoming floor votes as well as to build support for the party's positions on legislation.

Each party's leadership issues a formal public position on most, though not all, issues being considered by Congress, and some members of Congress, as one Hill insider observed, "are simply rubber stamps for whatever the leadership wants." A few in each party are mavericks, paying little attention to the leadership cue. As a congressman, Joe Schwarz became known as a "rather independent Republican," according to his legislative director, Chuck Yessaian, who went on to describe his new boss in the following terms: "He is a careful listener, and he always does listen to what the leadership wants...but he is absolutely not afraid to oppose the leadership. If an issue is not important to the congressman or to his district, he'll support the leadership. But if he feels strongly about something, he won't budge...regardless of what the leadership or anyone else might want."

The president is another actor in the constellation that makes up the universe of a member of Congress. "The White House weighs in on fewer issues than people typically think," a Hill staffer commented, "though when the administration does push a position, members of Congress have a variety of reactions. Some members of the president's party, for example, are scared of the White House's shadow, and absolutely will not vote against the president. For others, it is just another part of the mix."

Congressman Schwarz was certainly respectful of the White House, but he regarded the president's as just one of the chorus of voices that he wanted to take into consideration when making legislative decisions.

Interest groups often clamor to be heard as well, presenting an intriguing paradox in contemporary American politics. It has become a popular refrain in the complaints of commentators, disgruntled citizens, and reform-minded legislators that so-called special interests wield too much power in Washington. And it is certainly true that organized interests significantly influence policymaking, sometimes making headlines when pork-barrel spending reaches heights that raise eyebrows even in Washington or when bribery scandals involving members of Congress are uncovered. During Congressman Schwarz's freshman year, for example, Randy "Duke" Cunningham (R-Calif.) resigned from the House of Representatives after admitting that he had taken more than $2 million in bribes from defense contractors. But interest groups also serve several important purposes, such as raising public awareness on the issues they champion and providing information to legislators that is important to the decision-making process. Moreover, organized interests play a significant role in a representative democracy by amplifying the voices of average citizens, who join groups and associations that are relevant to their jobs or to particular concerns.

As Chuck Yessaian observed, "all members pay attention to interest groups at one time or another." Indeed, on some issues such groups are the most significant voices that a member of Congress must heed. "Obviously," Chuck noted, "there is variation from issue to issue, but really now... Michigan's congressional delegation cannot begin to ignore auto industry groups, or the National Association of Manufacturers. If they did, they wouldn't really be doing their jobs." The groups that are relevant to the Michigan Seventh are, as Chuck put it, "part of the mix," and their influence is a fact of life in Congress.

Finally, a congressman or -woman's own staff may prompt the boss to action, although as Yessaian points out, the extent to which the MC responds to staff cues is difficult to assess. "We make recommendations to the congressman from time to time," Chuck explained, adding with a laugh, "and the congressman listens to them from time to time. But," he continued, "staff will keep track of who is supporting which amendment to which bill, and every congressman, in every office is going to want that information. To that end, staff have influence by providing information that the member wants."

At the same time that the new member of Congress is learning how to take into account various demands from all of the actors in the congressional system, he or she must also learn the complex set of rules by which the legislative game is played. Freshmen need to know about different types of legislative initiatives—from bills, to resolutions, to concurrent and joint resolutions. They must also understand the process by which legislation is referred to standing committees. Sometimes, for example, a bill is divided up and sent to multiple committees; at other times, bill referral is affected by a perception that the chair of a particular committee will virtually guarantee a favorable (or unfavorable) hearing. In addition, new members in the House have to learn about the special and extremely important role played by the Rules Committee in moving bills toward consideration by the whole House, as well as about how legislation is scheduled for a hearing on the floor and what shortcuts may be taken with minor pieces of legislation. Eventually, a freshman must learn how to dislodge a bill that is stuck in committee. And, of course, if the member is to effectively participate in the legislative process, the variety and intricacy of floor procedures must be grasped. The arcane complexities of these rules of procedure cannot be digested quickly. That is why having some staff members with previous Hill experience is absolutely critical to a new MC's effectiveness in representing the interests of his or her constituents.

A system of calendars in the House allows for the categorization of bills. Freshmen legislators learn that the Union Calendar contains bills that raise or spend money, while the House Calendar includes bills that affect significant nonmonetary public measures. Less significant bills are put on the Corrections Calendar, and items such as claims against the government and immigration requests go on the Private Calendar. With staff help, a new member must learn when and under what conditions each calendar is called. He or she will also come to understand that there is no guarantee that simply because it is placed on a calendar, a bill will be debated on the floor.

New members also confront an intricate set of coordinating lights and bells that, at first, appears to have been designed merely to cause confusion. There are six lights on every clock on Capitol Hill, and a different meaning is attached to the number of lights that are illuminated at any one time. Three lights, for example, signal a quorum call. A *quorum*—the designated minimum number of members present—is necessary for conducting business on the floor of the chamber. Typically, members are not to be found there during most debates, but instead are in their offices or in committee meetings. Thus they need to be called to the floor when the official business of the House is to be conducted. Consequently, quorum calls can be used strategically, to slow down or speed up debate. If a quorum cannot be reached, the day's business ceases, to be continued the following day. When five lights on the clock are lit, on the other hand, members know that that a vote will be taken in fifteen minutes. When all six lights around the clock are lit, certain patterned cadences of bells go off at the same time, alerting members who may not be near a clock that a certain procedure is occurring on the floor. Quorum and vote calls bring a rush of legislators into the hallways. All elevators in the House office buildings become restricted—that is, "For Members Only"—so that congressmen and -women can get to the floor of the chamber quickly.

There is something charming about the lights and bells; they hark back to an era before Capitol Hill, like the rest of the country, was overtaken by modern technology. Lore has it that more than a century ago, the signal bells were also wired into taverns, hotels, and other places that were frequented during the day by members of Congress. Surely, more than one new legislator has echoed the puzzlement of Eddie Murphy's character in *The Distinguished Gentleman,* scratching his head while trying to follow the directives of the bells and the lights—even as messages coming in via email, pager, or BlackBerry are echoing the information that was once exclusively communicated by the congressional clocks.

From committee assignments, to caucus memberships, to voting cues, to House rules, members of Congress face a steep learning curve. They rely on each other and on their staffs to learn how to navigate the congressional system. As Congressman Schwarz was learning the ropes, the personnel roster in his Washington office was being finalized as well. Chuck Yessaian hired two additional legislative assistants to round out the Hill staff, one to pick up some of the substantive legislative work that the office was engaged in, and another, more senior person with a knowledge of military issues.

Chuck received nearly one hundred resumés for the more general LA position. His new hire had to have Capitol Hill experience; ties to Michigan would be a plus. Jared Page, who met both criteria, joined the staff in February 2005. Then twenty-five years old, Jared had grown up near the northern border of the Seventh District, in the town of Grand Ledge, and had earned a bachelors degree in political science and a masters in public policy, both from the University of Michigan. His first taste of politics had come during the summer of 2000, when, as an undergraduate, he worked for Joe Schwarz, who was then a state senator. Returning to school, Jared worked at the Gerald R. Ford Library in Ann Arbor, and then took a summer internship with a Washington lobbying firm before his last year at the university. While in D.C., Jared had made a number of contacts, including visits to the offices of the Michigan congressional delegation. Summer interns, Jared recalls with a smile, had engaged in a bit of competition to see who could get taken out to the greatest number of lunches, or who could collect the most business cards. Jared knew that he liked Washington, and he knew that he would be coming back.

After graduating from Michigan in 2003, Jared was ready to pound the pavement in Washington, looking for a job. His first stop was his congressman's office—Nick Smith from the Michigan Seventh. With a tone of understatement, Jared explains that he "got kind of lucky."

> The day I went into Congressman Smith's office, they said, "We have a staff opening, what do you think?" I said, "Yeah, I'm interested. Sure." Then they said, "OK, come in and meet the congressman." I'm thinking, "Like, whoa, this is going kinda fast. The congressman and I talked for a short

while, and then they said, "OK, you want a job?" I said, "Wow, can I think about it for a day?" They said, "Sure." The next day was Friday. I started the following Monday.

Timing is everything in politics, and Jared's was very good. Chuck appreciated Jared's experience on the Hill as well as his knowledge of the Seventh District. It was a bonus, of course, that he had also worked for Joe Schwarz in the past. Jared's resumé rose to the top, and he joined the new congressman's staff a couple of weeks after helping to close Nick Smith's office.

The second LA position, conferring the title Senior Legislative Assistant, required someone qualified to take on the responsibilities of working with Congressman Schwarz on his Armed Services Committee assignment. That meant having a detailed understanding of military matters and at least the potential for receiving the security clearance necessary for working with the classified information that came to Armed Services. Having received approximately fifty applications for this position, Chuck interviewed about six candidates. Finally, as Chuck put it, he "stepped outside the box a bit on Aaron's hire—a senior LA with no Hill experience is rather unconventional." In his mid-thirties, Aaron Taliaferro had completed nearly ten years of active service in the air force, and then had become a specialist in cost analysis and finance. He brought a well-honed sense of how weapons systems are researched and developed, of how they are "costed out," and of the steps that lead to weapons deployment. Aaron had worked directly with Secretary of Defense Donald Rumsfeld, and he had the highest security clearance one could get. Chuck also thought that Aaron would fit in well with the rest of the Schwarz office staff, which he joined in mid-April 2005.

A little more than twelve weeks since the Swearing-In, Congressman Schwarz's office was up and running. The tasks and legislative policy areas had been divided among the staff, each of whom had multiple responsibilities. As the chart shows, there was plenty of work for everyone.

As the staff became immersed in various issue areas and as the congressman began to learn the nuances of the congressional process, there was the district to be attended to, travel and speaking schedules to meet, votes to cast...and an election campaign that was only a year away.

Joe Schwarz's Washington Staff

Name	Office Tasks and Legislative Policy Areas
Matt Marsden *chief of staff*	Press calls, federal appointments
Chuck Yessaian *legislative director*	Appropriations, special projects, filtering all issues to the congressman
Rob Blackwell *special assistant*	Director of interns, scheduling coordination, emergency coordination, bodyman
Mark Ratner *legislative assistant*	Telecommunications technology, Internet technology, health, social issues, Social Security, education, labor, federal employee issues, pensions, manufacturing
Louie Meizlish *legislative assistant*	Transportation issues, infrastructure issues, judiciary and Second Amendment issues, immigration, international relations, taxes, budget, civil rights, trade, tours*
Meghan Kolassa *legislative assistant*	Agriculture, housing, animal rights, postal issues, small business, ethics, government reform, House administration
Jared Page *legislative assistant*	Science, environment, interior, Great Lakes, energy/nuclear waste, arts, insurance, banking, flag requests*
Aaron Taliaferro *senior legislative assistant*	Military, homeland security, first responders, veterans

*constituent service activities

Representation
You Know It When You See It

ANY EIGHTH GRADER who has done his or her social studies homework has some notion of the responsibility of members of Congress to represent their constituents. When pressed by a teacher to explain what it means to "represent" someone, a likely response is, "You know, like, doing what people want or tell you to do." Further probing of the meaning of the term is probably going to result in an unspoken "Oh…leave me alone."

A college student who is asked to define *representation* might suggest that a member of Congress should be working to pass legislation that is in line with the policy preferences of the people he or she is supposed to be representing. When pressed by a professor to explain who these constituents are, or how a congressman or -woman knows what their preferences are, or how choices are made among competing preferences, however, a roomful of students in an American government class or in a legislative process course will most likely be unable to agree on any single definition of the term.

Ironically, there was no mention of representation in the big binders given to Joe Schwarz during his orientation sessions on Capitol Hill or at Harvard. Even as he was being introduced to the ways of the House of *Representatives,* and was soon to take the oath of office and become *Representative* Schwarz, there was no discussion of what representation is, or how it is done. Perhaps defining this concept is akin to Justice Potter Stewart's famous observation about obscenity: "I shall not today attempt further to define the kinds of material I understand to be embraced within that shorthand description, and perhaps I could never succeed in intelligibly doing so. But I know it when I see it."[1] So, when does Joe Schwarz—or any of his 434 colleagues in the House—feel that he is representing his district? Which tasks or actions constitute representation? When do constituents feel that they have been represented? What demands for representation do people make? What does it mean to be a member of the House of Representatives?

Representation is, in fact, a slippery concept—one that political scientists have examined in a variety of theoretical and empirical ways. Over time, several views have been offered about how a legislator should perform the representation function.[2] One perspective is that representatives should be *trustees* of the broad interests of the nation, acting on the basis of their own convictions and sound judgments when making decisions about legislative matters. A second view holds that legislators should behave as *delegates*, taking cues from their constituents and reflecting the opinions of those they represent. Rather than following the dictates of their consciences as trustees do, delegates act on the basis of what they feel they have been instructed to do.

A third view of the representational role, which has been labeled the *politico*, describes a legislator who moves back and forth between the trustee and delegate models, depending on the issue. This flexibility factor suggests that when the folks back home care a lot about an issue and make their views known, the legislator will act as a delegate. However, at other times—when there is no consensus or clear-cut view emerging from the constituency, or when the legislator believes that with respect to a particular issue, the broad interests of society should carry more weight—the legislator will act as a trustee. Furthermore, legislators may sometimes feel a responsibility to make decisions that are in keeping with the positions their political parties have taken. When adopting the role of the *partisan*, the representative takes direction from the party leadership in determining his or her position on legislative issues.[3]

These models—trustee, delegate, politico, and partisan—provide a useful starting point for thinking about the ways in which legislators fulfill their representational function. What about the people they represent?

From a constituent's perspective, it is perhaps easiest to think that representation "happens" when your member of Congress supports a policy position that you agree with, or votes as you wish him to, adopting the role of the delegate. But does that mean you are not being represented when your MC casts a vote that is not in keeping with your views or takes a stand on an issue that you disagree with? In refining the concept of representation, political scientists have suggested that one member of the House of Representatives cannot represent all of the several hundred thousand constituents in a district. Rather, the collectivity of all 435 House members is likely to reflect viewpoints held by millions of constituents across the country. Thus, while you may not be best "represented" by your particular member of Congress, you are likely to be represented by someone.[4]

While scholars have employed a number of conceptual and empirical approaches to understanding representation, the focus of study, for the most part, has been on the decisions legislators make with respect to policy. But is policy congruence—either between a congressman or -woman and his or her district or between any member of Congress and any constituent—a satisfactory measurement of representation? Is taking a stand on policy or casting a vote, whether as trustee, delegate, or partisan, all that should be considered when thinking about representation? How do all of the other activities that legislators engage in, beyond taking a stand on policy, relate to being a *representative?* What exactly did Chuck Yessaian, Congressman Schwarz's legislative director, mean when he told his newly-assembled staff, "At the end of the day, it's all about the constituents"? What is *it?*

Over most of the past hundred years, members of Congress have engaged in a mix of activities that include lawmaking, pork-barreling, and casework.[5] *Lawmaking,* of course, has to do with taking positions on, sponsoring, and voting on legislative matters. *Pork-barreling* refers to efforts to bring tangible benefits to the district. The economic impact of water-treatment projects, road repairs, or federal buildings is not lost on the folks back home.

The third activity, *casework,* is the provision of favors and services that members of Congress can offer to their constituents. Intervening to find a lost Social Security check, speeding up the process for obtaining a passport, or helping with an emergency leave for a member of the armed forces are some of the services that congressional offices routinely provide for people in the district. Casework links members of Congress and federal bureaucratic agencies in a special way, as MCs and their staffs rely on these agencies to help them deliver the needed services to their constituents. A reciprocal bond is formed when these same agencies come before Congress each year, seeking funding, as well as authorizations for new programs, as part of the annual budget appropriations process. Because each needs the other, Congress and the bureaucracy work together to provide constituent services. Moreover, as the scope of the federal government has grown and bureaucratic red tape has increased, so too has the amount of time spent on casework. In fact, casework activity probably takes up as much time as lawmaking and pork-barreling combined.

If the congressional job description includes so much constituent casework, and also involves "bringing home the bacon"—in the form of funding for projects that benefit the district—does it make sense to view representation as primarily a matter of taking positions on public policy? Are concepts of representation that focus on the role of a member of Congress as a trustee or a delegate or something in between a bit too restrictive? In point of fact, members of the House of Representatives perform a dizzying array of tasks, some of which have to do with making decisions about weighty legislative issues, to be sure. But they also help those they "represent" with individual needs and concerns, and at times, they engage in actions that are primarily symbolic, such as offering resolutions on behalf of the district or making site visits to new schools or businesses in the district. Does representation encompass all of these activities? Taking a look at what a member of Congress does and listening to what he says about the business of representation allows us to link a practical view to the more conceptual treatments.

New to Congress, Representative Schwarz found that his job as a legislator included a wide range of activities. He put out numerous policy statements, made public announcements about his participation in meetings in the district that focused on substantive issues, and took actions directly related to legislation. He also engaged in a number of activities that carried symbolic overtones. In addition, members of the congressman's staff—and occasionally the congressman himself—were providing constituent casework services, and Schwarz's office made numerous announcements about federal grants that had been awarded to various entities in Michigan's Seventh District.

Indeed, much of Representative Schwarz's workload in the early going involved tasks that correspond to the view of representation as focused on policy. He made a number of public statements and took action on issues of national concern as well as on topics that had more direct significance to his district. Three months after taking office, for example, Schwarz spoke in favor of the Head Start program, and, a couple of weeks later, he spoke out against cuts in Medicaid funding. He also issued statements on the 2005 Defense Appropriations Bill and the war in Iraq.

Other actions were also part of the policy representation mix. On February 10, 2005—just five weeks after taking office—Congressman Schwarz signed on as a cosponsor of a bipartisan bill (HR 310, 109th Cong.) to raise the fines on broadcasters who violate decency standards, from $32,500 to $500,000. In a statement announcing his support for this legislation, Schwarz said, "The fines as they exist are not a deterrent to broadcasters who air indecent materials. If these broadcasters are unable to make the right choice and refrain from airing material that is offensive or inappropriate, then we must raise the fine for indecent broadcasts to a level that they can no longer ignore." In the early spring, he made public statements and cast votes on energy, family farm relief, the repeal of the "death tax," and a variety of defense issues. As the year unfolded, his office made the public aware of his votes on a Homeland Security measure and on a House-Senate compromise for funding operations in Iraq. Dr. Schwarz's concern with health care was also evident in public statements and in votes. He supported increased health benefits for military reservists and their families, and he voted to increase medical care for veterans.

Congressman Schwarz spoke with satisfaction about one occasion on which a small, bipartisan group of members of the Armed Services Committee met early one morning with the committee's chairman and

...just batted the ball around about what we could do, that we're not doing, to help the troops. We have troops in Iraq, Afghanistan, other places...are we doing enough to fund research on combating Improvised Explosive Devices (IEDs)? Is medical care for troops coming home as good as we want it to be? What can we do to make it better? To improve facilities? What can we do to make certain that people who leave the service, who have health problems as a result of their service—whether it's a psychiatric problem or long-term treatment of wounds—have the care they need? What can be done to better serve them?

After that 8:00 a.m. informal meeting, Schwarz and his colleagues went into an open hearing of the full Armed Services Committee, where they heard from the commander of the Afghanistan operation; a closed hearing followed. "By the end of the morning," Congressman Schwarz recalled, "we had a pretty good idea of what was going on and how we could help things out." There was a great deal of satisfaction in his voice as he spoke about foreign and military policy, and the way that his engagement with these issues was directly linked to his representational responsibilities.

On that same day, Joe met with the Tuesday Group, where the discussion centered on a bill before the House to allow oil drilling on the Arctic Continental Shelf. The group's members had been startled to see an editorial in that morning's *Washington Post* supporting the legislation, given the more typical liberal leanings on environmental and social issues in the *Post*'s opinion pages. Like many of the moderates who make up the Tuesday Group, Representative Schwarz was a friend of the environment, and he described the group's resistance to the original proposal in positive terms:

> The Tuesday Group thought the bill was so imperfect that we decided we would withhold our support unless changes were made. We really had an effect there...the thirty or so members of the group made it clear that we would withhold votes and the bill's sponsors and party leadership would not have enough support to pass the bill. Many of the changes we wanted were made overnight—enough so that twenty or so of us could support it.

Schwarz took satisfaction in playing a role in making changes (in his view, for the better) to the legislation, contending that such input constitutes a significant aspect of the representation function.

On other occasions, the congressman continued to stand by his convictions on environmental issues. Schwarz went public with a statement that took the Bush administration and many congressional Republicans to task for their proposal to drill for oil in the Arctic National Wildlife Refuge (ANWR). Even when the freshman congressman received a visit from Interior Secretary Gale Norton, he didn't back down. In the meeting, Schwarz responded to this official pressure by reiterating his opposition:

> This is a cabinet officer, setting up an appointment to come to my office to talk. She came by to personally ask me to support drilling in ANWR. I was delighted to meet with her—she is very charming and very bright—and I told her that there was no way I would support drilling in ANWR. I told her that a program to allow such drilling was the poster child for more harvesting natural resources, not only from public lands, but in this case a wildlife refuge... and I just don't want to do that.

When the legislative battle over the issue erupted in December 2005, Congressman Schwarz was not shy about entering the fray. Senator Ted Stevens (R-Alaska), whose state stood to reap considerable financial benefits from the project, attached a drilling proposal to a defense-spending bill that was before the Senate and would certainly be considered in the House. In response, Congressman Schwarz was quoted in the press— calling it "utterly despicable to be put in a position of choosing between funding our troops and opposing bad public policy."[6]

Congressman Schwarz's defiance of the initiative of a senior senator in his own party generated a significant amount of public support, including several approving letters to the editor from constituents that appeared in local newspapers. In addition, the president of the League of Conservation Voters wrote a letter to the newspapers in the district, declaring, "We applaud U.S. Representative Joe Schwarz," the letter began, "for his leadership in fighting to protect the Arctic National Wildlife Refuge."[7]

Joe's commitment to the environment was demonstrated once more when, again voting against his party, he opposed the Threatened and Endangered Species Recovery Act of 2005, which, he claimed, would "effectively gut the Endangered Species Act." Schwarz also voiced his support for a court decision disallowing the Environmental Protection Agency from exempting ship operators from clean-water regulations in their disposal of the ballast water that maintains a ship's stability. In his statement, Schwarz noted that such water (which contains a substance that is a pollutant) is a threat to the Great Lakes ecosystem.

Other issues that Joe addressed also resonated in the Michigan Seventh. He spoke about a mission being undertaken by a National Guard unit from the district, for instance, and issued a public statement about the prospect of opening up the Japanese market for beef—a subject of critical importance to a district with agricultural interests. Congressman Schwarz also voted in support of Amtrak funding, and in praising the House for passing this legislation, he noted that the funding was of critical importance to the jobs of countless residents of Michigan's Seventh District and to the thousands of passengers boarding Amtrak every year in southern Michigan. (There was no mention of the use of locomotives as weapons to hunt wild turkeys, as discussed in chapter 2.)

Another issue of direct concern to his constituents was a Schwarz amendment to the Agricultural Appropriations Bill for 2006 (a measure that was passed in 2005). The amendment directed the Department of Agriculture to prioritize the eradication of the emerald ash borer, an exotic insect that has damaged millions of ash trees in Michigan and other states in the Midwest. In this case, Congressman Schwarz showed some legislative creativity by enlisting Major League Baseball (MLB) to lobby in support of his amendment. MLB got in the game because Louisville Slugger, a supplier of bats to both the American and National Leagues, depends heavily on the ash trees that are threatened by what Dr. Schwarz called "this horrible beetle."

Like all members of Congress, Schwarz also met with various groups when he was back in the district. At those times, it was not at all uncommon to find him conducting Q & A sessions in a union or grange hall, listening to the views of his constituents on the policy issues that matter

On his weekly visits to the district, Congressman Schwarz met frequently with members of the farming community, both to keep this constituency abreast of his work on the Agriculture Committee and to update his own understanding of farm issues and needs back home.

most to them. In 2005 he made considerable efforts to meet with members of the farming community in order to gather information and exchange ideas that would be helpful to his work on the Agriculture Committee. Some of these meetings were highlighted on the congressman's Web site.

Two specific policy issues consumed a great deal of the new congressman's time during 2005. One involved the list of military bases that the Department of Defense was considering for closure or relocation. Schwarz was committed to fighting for two important facilities in Battle Creek. The second policy area touched the medical professional in the congressman, who became heavily involved in the push by moderate Republicans to support stem-cell research. (These two issues are fully considered in chapter 7.)

Reports of Congressman Schwarz's actions on legislation covering a wide range of areas, his statements on public policy, and notices of his meetings with constituent groups about substantive issues were circulated to all of the media outlets in the district, allowing constituents to take a measure of their representative's policy views on both a national and a local scale. Schwarz evidenced frustration, however, in pointing out that in his view, certain actions that are taken in Congress are not related to representation:

> Some days, because of the schedule, we are forced to deal with things that I don't think are substantive. An example would be when the leadership feels they need to appease the base, so we have conversations and sometimes resolutions espousing one position or another on social issues. With a war going on in Iraq and Afghanistan, the economy not so wonderful in the state of Michigan, with health care in crisis, with environmental issues that need to be dealt with. ... When I have to go vote on these other kinds of things, it's a damn waste of time.

The congressman himself was also involved in activities that were, perhaps, less substantive and more symbolic in nature.[8] His cosponsorship of a resolution urging President Bush to direct the U.S. ambassador to the United Nations to work for further reduction of anti-Semitic language and anti-Israel resolutions at the UN is illustrative of symbolic

Early in his term, Schwarz traveled to the military base at Guantanamo Bay, Cuba, where detainees considered terrorist threats were housed. The visit helped to inform Joe's work on the House Armed Services Committee.

representation. Similarly, his public comment on the death of the pope—"As a Catholic layperson, I was deeply saddened to learn of the passing of Pope John Paul II. I was a great admirer of his, and I join the world community in mourning his passing."—is the sort of action that falls into the category of symbolic representation.

Symbolism is important in American politics, and governmental leaders are expected to engage in such activities and to issue such statements to the national audience—or to the world. But, reflecting the adage that "All politics is local," members of Congress sometimes make symbolic statements that have a distinctly regional flavor. On June 13, 2005, Schwarz and his colleague from Michigan's Sixth District, Fred Upton, spoke on the House floor to honor the life of Thurl Arthur Ravenscroft, whose passing Joe noted as that of "a friend and neighbor" to all in southern Michigan. Memorializing Ravenscroft, who was associated with numerous animated characters, as "the voice of Tony the Tiger, the orange and black striped spokesman for Kellogg's Frosted Flakes," Joe concluded, "Southern Michigan will not be the same without Thurl Ravenscroft. He was GRRRREEEEAT!" Less imaginative, perhaps, but more commonplace, were Congressman Schwarz's appearances at a number of events in the district, such as the opening of an exhibit on "Children and the Holocaust" at the Art Center of Battle Creek.

No less symbolic was Joe's meeting with the ambassador of Serbia and the Serbian defense minister at his Hill office. In recounting this meeting, Joe suppressed a self-satisfied chuckle as he reported that "the ambassador is a graduate of the University of Michigan." Joe continued, "The new Serbia, the really new Serbia, (since it's not Serbia and Montenegro anymore), is really looking to the West. ... They want to join the European Union (EU) and ultimately, NATO." In this instance, even a freshman legislator can be seen as playing the role of statesman, symbolizing the national government to foreign leaders.

As noted earlier, bureaucratic agencies and members of Congress have a relationship that is based, to some extent, on mutual need: the bureaucracy needs Congress for funding, and Congress needs the bureaucracy for the provision of services and programs. A public manifestation of this cooperative relationship sometimes arose in the federal grant process. When, for example, a grant to fund a study or a program or a facility was made by an agency within the Department of Health and Human Services (HHS) to a university or a company or a health provider in Michigan's Seventh Congressional District, HHS would notify Congressman Schwarz as well as Michigan's U.S. senators before the grant recipient learned of the award. In some instances, the representative or one of the senators might have been instrumental in obtaining the grant for a constituent. Oftentimes, however, a member of Congress would simply announce, by way of a press release, that a grant had been awarded. The legislator was thus publicly associated with the financial support coming from Washington to the district, even though he or she had had nothing to do with the process. Politicians are not shy about announcing these federal grants; Congressman Schwarz made nearly three dozen such announcements during his freshman year. In doing so, he was engaging in a form of representation—connecting the federal government to the folks back home—that has grown in importance as the nexus between Congress and the bureaucracy has become more significant.

The link between members of Congress and the bureaucracy has given rise to another essential part of a representative's job description—constituent casework.

When pressed to explain what he meant when he told his staff that "it's all about the constituents," Chuck Yessaian responded emphatically: "You have to help your constituents out. … You must respond as quickly as possible to their questions…you cannot ignore them." Furthermore, he continued, "Every office on the Hill helps constituents with personal problems and issues. In fact, every office is set up to do this. We serve an ombudsman function and we know it. It is part of the job description here."

The importance of constituent casework was not lost on Congressman Schwarz. "You cannot run an effective congressional office unless you are very good at dealing with constituent matters," he observed. "In fact, you could make the argument that Congress has acceded to itself, probably by default, the function of universal ombudsman on federal matters. This has happened over the last forty or fifty years as the federal bureaucracy has grown. Everyone is connected to the bureaucracy at the hip, in one way or another."

The congressman not only regarded constituent casework as a major part of his job, but also saw it as an important element of his representational responsibilities. "You spend a huge amount of time on it," Schwarz explained. "The people in the district offices and in Washington are working on constituent things all the time—*all* the time—and they are remarkably good at it. In fact, they are wizards at it." Schwarz viewed his staff as central to casework, describing each of them in terms of their constituency responsibilities:

I have one person who does nothing but deal with veterans issues, and another who deals with other federal benefit issues. I have one person who deals with nothing but agricultural issues, because the district is so intensively agricultural. My military legislative assistant not only does the policy stuff, but also deals with things having to do with military families and issues that they have while a family member is away on active duty. . . . The staff is dealing with constituent issues all day, everyday.

The congressman himself got personally involved in some constituent matters. Sometimes, a staff member would come to him, indicating that he or she thought a constituent had a reasonable case but could not quite convince the appropriate bureaucratic office. Joe explained, "A staff member might say, 'I just can't crack the bureaucracy, I'm almost there, but a call from you, Congressman, will put it over the top.' Hell," Joe continued, "I'll make the call, and we'll get it done."

Representative Schwarz derived considerable satisfaction from some of this casework, admitting,

> Some of the ones I love involve World War II veterans. Sometimes it's the family of a deceased individual, and the family cannot find his medals. You love to be helpful in those situations. A lot of times it's about people who are still alive. My high school biology teacher is a good example. He served with distinction in the China-Burma-India theater, in the army air force, and just had his 90th birthday. His medals had been misplaced somewhere along the line. I became personally involved in that. We did everything we could and we were able to get the medals replaced. You just love to help people in that way.

He also became personally involved in other casework having to do with the military, including the situation of a navy enlisted man—the son of a nurse Joe had met at the university health system in Ann Arbor— who wanted to stay in the navy and be an officer. After reviewing the sailor's record and meeting with him in the Washington office, Joe called the navy liaison to the House and persuaded him to work with this fellow personally, to get him started in Naval Officers Candidate School. Joe's sense of satisfaction at the result of his intervention in this matter was evident: "I'll bet he gets commissioned. I love to get involved with that kind of stuff."

Congressman Schwarz saw constituent service for what it is—a fact of congressional life and a significant part of the job description. The ability to help constituents with their individual needs, moreover, is one of the essential advantages of incumbents when it comes time to stand for reelection. Challengers are simply not in a position to cut through the bureaucratic maze of Washington on behalf of the people in the district, while members of Congress are uniformly willing to commit considerable staff time to servicing the district through casework. By word of mouth, news of favors provided by members of Congress gets around.[9]

Indeed, because members of Congress always have to cast an eye toward the next election, they must continuously engage in activities that relate to reelection—credit claiming, advertising, and position taking.[10] *Credit claiming* is important to members of Congress. If voters believe that a representative can make good things happen, it is logical to assume that they will want to keep that representative in office. Clearly, constituent casework is critical to credit claiming. So, too, is announcing the federal grants that have been awarded to institutions and organizations in the district, and, of course, bringing tangible benefits to the constituency through earmarks or pork-barrel legislation. *Advertising* encompasses appearances at district events, letters of congratulation, and other ways of creating a favorable image. There is little issue content in these activities—they are the stuff of symbolic politics. *Position taking,* which involves directly confronting the issues, may take the form of bill sponsorship, votes, policy statements, press releases, or meetings about substantive issues with the folks back home. Members of Congress believe that their issue positions make a difference that is likely to be reflected in election returns.

All these activities, then, are essential to the electoral process; they also reflect the mix of activities that make up the representational function. The framers intended the lower chamber of Congress to represent the people as a whole. Unlike the Senate, the president, or members of the Supreme Court, members of the House were to be directly elected.[11] Thus, the House of Representatives is at the core of American representative democracy, a system of government in which the people elect individuals to make decisions on their behalf. Systematic, fair elections are held to choose political leaders—representatives—who will hold office for a specified period of time. Theoretically, if a sufficient number of voters are satisfied with the way they have been represented by an incumbent, that representative remains in office to serve another term. Again, according to democratic theory, if the voters determine that their congressman or -woman has not done a good job of representation, the bid for reelection fails, and a new representative is put into office. Thus the business of representation, in all of its facets—policymaking on a grand scale, provision of benefits to the district, constituent casework, and even symbolic action—are inextricably tied to electoral politics. In the end, members of the House of Representatives, "the People's House," work for and are accountable to those they represent.

Meanwhile, Back in the District

It is 566 miles from Jackson, Michigan, to Washington, D.C. On the eight-hour drive, one passes through Toledo, Cleveland, Youngstown, Pittsburgh, and Baltimore. There were days when it seemed to Rebecca Schneider, district director for Congressman Schwarz, that Capitol Hill was worlds away from Michigan's Seventh Congressional District. There were other times when she was in such close contact with the Washington office that she felt as though she, too, were in D.C.

A pleasant, outgoing woman in her mid-thirties, Rebecca was in charge of the congressman's three district offices and the staffers who worked in them. She laughingly says of herself, "I'm living proof that the blind resumé works." In 1997, armed with an undergraduate degree from Kalamazoo College and a master's degree in public administration from George Washington University, Rebecca had sent her resumé to every Republican in the Michigan state senate. As it happened, Joe Schwarz's office had an opening. Rebecca smiles at the recollection of how she was hired: "His chief of staff had already drafted the 'please go away, leave us alone and don't bother us again' letter and Schwarz was about to sign it. But then he flipped through my application and resumé and said, 'Wait, let's get her in here—I'd like to meet her.' I stayed with Joe until he was term-limited out of the Michigan senate."

After her time with Schwarz in the state legislature, Rebecca worked for the state's attorney general, Mike Cox, and then served a brief stint in the Government Relations office of the Karmanos Cancer Institute in Detroit. When Joe announced his candidacy for Congress in 2004,

Rebecca was glad to help with the campaign. Her connection to the Schwarz operation, however, "caused the most stressful time in my marriage." As it happened, Rebecca's husband Matthew was the chairman of the Washtenaw County Republican Party, and he had endorsed Gene DeRossett in the August 2004 Republican primary before Schwarz entered the race. DeRossett was offended, to put it mildly, that the wife of the county party chairman was supporting another candidate. Nor was that support a secret—the Schneider house was, after all, the site of one of Senator John McCain's campaign stops for Joe Schwarz during the primary. Peace was later restored, but there was a period of very prickly relations between DeRossett and the Schneiders.

Despite the conflict, Rebecca was eager to work for Joe again. A self-described "believer," she genuinely agreed with his politics and thought his voice and viewpoint should be part of the political discourse. As she put it, "Working for the congressman is more than just a paycheck." She was, however, a bit unsure how to approach Joe. She thought it was inappropriate to say anything before the general election, and she was concerned about stepping on Matt Marsden's toes. Even though Rebecca had worked her way up to being Schwarz's chief of staff in the Michigan state senate, she was assuming nothing.

After the November election, she decided to ask a close friend of Joe's to "feel things out, and to find out what the plan was for Matt." When the friend reported that the Schwarz camp was not quite sure what Marsden was going to do, she let it be known, through that same friend, that she was interested in being district director. When she learned that Joe would be glad to speak with her, Rebecca called him up and said, "Hey, I'd love to work for you again, and if you have room for me, I hope you'll consider me." As Rebecca reported it, they met soon after their phone call, and the ensuing conversation focused on sorting out the details of salary and seniority. Rebecca notes with a chuckle,

> I never really had an interview, and I hope I wasn't shoved down anyone's throat by the boss. Frankly, I don't think chief of staff was Matt's first choice... but, I sat down with the congressman and Matt when they were transitioning from the campaign office to the congressional office. We talked about what kind of salary I would need. They said they could do

that, and that was about it. As I remember the meeting, we then moved on—the three of us—and talked about who would be placed in what spot, and how much we could offer each person. We had people who had worked on the campaign and they had to be placed in the positions we had. Those were their expectations, and ours.

As soon as she signed on with the congressman, Rebecca had some rather pressing matters to handle. The first was to find suitable spaces for the district offices. The former congressman, Nick Smith, had maintained two district offices. Both of them—Jackson, in the eastern part of the Seventh District, and Battle Creek, in the western part—were in population centers that were accessible from I-94. The Schwarz operation wanted an additional office in a somewhat centralized location in the northwestern section of the district so that constituents from towns such as Charlotte and Vermontville were not faced with a one-and-a-half-hour drive to Battle Creek if they needed help from the congressman's staff. The fact that the area around Delta Township constituted part of Joe's state senate district also played into the decision to locate an office there. Even before Rebecca was hired, Joe and Matt began negotiating for a space to serve that area of nearly 30,000 people. The space they rented was a lovely old house on Saginaw Highway, a main thoroughfare in suburban Lansing; its rooms allowed for five nice-sized offices, in addition to a front room that served as a welcome and waiting area and provided ample space for office equipment. Because the property was owned by an acquaintance of the congressman, the Schwarz operation was able to rent the facility at a very favorable rate.

In Battle Creek, the decision about where to locate an office was easy—Congressman Schwarz simply moved into the space vacated by the retiring congressman, Nick Smith. The property owner understood the functions of a congressional district office and was glad for the uninterrupted tenancy. Moreover, the storefront space was quite close to a senior citizens center; continuing to house a district office there meant that these constituents, who tend to be quite active and often avail themselves of the services of their representative, would not have to become familiar with a new address. In fact, the Schwarz campaign had occupied space in the same building, so the choice made sense for number of reasons. The space

The storefront of the Schwarz office in Battle Creek, Michigan.

rented for $1,500 per month and was outfitted with an office in back, two workstations in front, and a conference room.

Finding office space in Jackson, which offered few suitable choices to house a district office, was more challenging. Rebecca enlisted the help of Jeane Johnson, a tireless senior citizen and longtime Schwarz supporter, who, according to Rebecca, knew "everything there is to know about Jackson." Jeane's prominence in local Republican politics reflected both her roots and her connectedness: her father had been a state legislator, Jeane herself had been the first female page in the Michigan state legislature, and her husband had served as a county commissioner. Working with a local commercial realtor, Jeane quickly learned that there were plenty of spaces to buy, but not to rent, in Jackson. Also, the Schwarz team's desire to locate in the downtown area eliminated from consideration a strip-mall area on the outskirts of Jackson, even though it offered more plentiful options. Rebecca and Jeane looked at four spaces, including a former striptease joint, which Rebecca rejected because it might not send the appropriate message. They settled instead on a $2,000 per month storefront on Mechanic Street that accommodated a conference room, an office for the congressman when he was in Jackson, and four additional work areas.

As Rebecca went about setting up and staffing the various district offices, she knew that it was going to take some time to feel a sense of rhythm and routine in her life. There were computers and furniture to buy, and some construction was necessary in the Jackson office. People wanted to get to work, but, as Rebecca put it, "It's hard to feel productive when you don't have a desk, a phone, or a computer." The Schwarz team had to invent new systems for most activities, and Rebecca predicted that it would take at least a couple of months to feel settled. Looking back on those early days in the district, Rebecca remembers working in her office as construction was going on around her. She picked up a cell-phone call from Matt Marsden. "Hey," Matt said, "this senior staff thing is great… very glamorous. I'm taking a break from painting my office." Rebecca laughed knowingly and replied, "I've got you beat. I just finished cleaning the toilet in the Jackson office."

In addition to her custodial responsibilities, Rebecca had to assign various office positions to campaign staffers who had been promised jobs if Schwarz won, hire some new staff members, and divide up constituent service issue areas across the staff in the three district offices. Also, in the back of her mind—though not very far back—was the admonition she had received from Jeane Johnson during the week immediately following Joe's election: "Come on, let's get going… what are we doing about this, this, and this…? There's just 23½ months until the next election."

Given the heavily agricultural nature of the Seventh District, Rebecca knew that she would need an agriculture expert in one of the district offices. After interviewing several candidates, Rebecca found, "the choice was easy." Rob Glazier had worked for the Michigan Department of Agriculture, and his background included work on the impact of various fertilizers and chemicals in groundwater in the agricultural arena. In his early thirties, Rob had a bachelor's degree in political science from the University of Michigan—a fact that no doubt pleased the congressman—

and he had done volunteer work for the Schwarz campaign. One of the first people hired to work in the district, Rob was assigned to the Jackson office to work alongside Rebecca and Jeane Johnson.

Jeane was named outreach coordinator, from which post she would keep in close contact with various groups in the district, learning about their needs and letting them know that the Schwarz organization would work with them. Shortly after the new year began, Deanna Wiltse joined the Jackson staff to do clerical work, answer the phones, and greet constituents when they came into the office. Deanna, who had been working as a "temp" in the Blackman Township office, was recommended to Rebecca by a Schwarz supporter in that area. A friendly, outgoing young woman, Deanna became a kind of gatekeeper, directing callers to the appropriate staffer in the congressman's local offices.

The Delta Township office staff included a middle-aged, soft-spoken native of Texas, Faye Armstrong, who had moved to Michigan with her husband, a native Michigander, in 1988. Taking a job as a scheduler in a state senate office, she had come to know Joe Schwarz during his tenure in that body. Faye later went to work for then governor John Engler, holding a number of positions on the governor's staff over a ten-year period. After that, she spent two years as executive assistant to the chairman of the state Republican Party and, while there, was invited to join the Schwarz team. Faye was given the responsibility of managing and coordinating Congressman Schwarz's schedule. A member of Congress must adhere to a complicated calendar, on which there are frequently competing demands on a member's time. In Rebecca's estimation, Faye handled the scheduling issues adroitly: "She knows how to say no, and say it very nicely. She is always lovely to people, but is always in control. We all talk to Faye daily, and frankly, we should all be thanking her daily."

Initially, the Delta office also housed Paul Egnatuk and Cheryl Chapko. Paul, who had been very active in the congressional campaign, was designated manager of the Delta operation. Cheryl had worked on a state senator's staff, and, when he was term-limited out of the statehouse, she had taken the early retirement package that was made available to state employees. As an old friend of Rebecca's, however, she was delighted to return to the workforce by joining Congressman Schwarz's district staff.

Above, the constituent operation in Delta Township, Michigan, just outside Lansing. Left, Faye Armstrong, who handled long-term scheduling for the congressman.

Two young women who had done work on the congressional campaign—Danielle Moreland and Danielle Miller (the "Danielles")—became staffers in the Battle Creek office. Moreland, who had worked for a number of candidates throughout the state of Michigan and lived near Battle Creek, was well-known in the state's Republican circles. Miller had been a student at Albion College when she joined the Schwarz campaign.

By the end of February 2005, Rebecca was still heavily engaged in the process of setting up the offices. Much of January had been spent in getting the technology side of the Jackson office up and running. The computers that had once been used by the staff of the former congress-man, Nick Smith, were woefully out of date, so new equipment had to be purchased and formatted. Rebecca was also frustrated with the unreliable phone and Internet service—the service provider for the Delta office was reluctant to admit that Jackson was somewhere between the fringe of its service area and outside of it completely. After weeks of dissatisfaction, a new phone and Internet provider was found in the needed area, and the Jackson office finally went online.

A software program designed for government officials was selected by the Washington staff and purchased for use in both the district and D.C. offices. The package, *Capitol Correspond*, facilitates the tracking of phone calls, constituent opinion, and all incoming and outgoing mail; it also helps with the generation of press releases, the management of casework files, the processing of requests from constituents, and general daily office management. A fair amount of staff training had to take place before everyone felt comfortable using it, but the software proved to be valuable in managing the constant flow of communication between constituents and the district offices. The Schwarz district staff opened 50–75 cases (specific constituent requests for help) per month and logged between 500 and 1,000 discrete constituent opinions per month. Those opinions came in the form of phone calls, letters, or emails.

Throughout February, the Jackson office still suffered from a shortage of furniture. Rebecca was using as her desk a makeshift piece inherited from former Congressman Smith, and the office that had been designated for Congressman Schwarz's use remained largely unfurnished. The con-ference room, however, was functional, and Rebecca was pleased that there was a suitable space where the congressman could meet with visi-tors and constituents.

Although the logistical concerns of setting up the district offices occu-pied much of her time in the early months of Joe's first year in the House, Rebecca also had to deal with some fundamental issues related to running a congressional district operation. She distributed a list of substantive constituent service issue areas and invited every member of the district staff to choose one issue area to cover. Her goal was to give everyone at least one issue that he or she wanted. "I have no clue what led most of the staff to think that immigration would be one of the easier issues to work with," Rebecca reflected on the process with a grin. The initial configuration assigned agriculture and immigration to the Jackson office, Medicare and IRS issues to Delta, and veterans' issues and Social Security to Battle Creek. In addition to these major categories, the staff also divided up more specific tasks, including the following items:

Military academy
   appointments
Postal service
Legal concerns
Federal retirement benefits
Local government disaster
   assistance and federal
   compliance
Small business issues
Environment
Student issues (such as
   loans and financial aid)

Award certificates and tributes
Government contracts
Grants
Department of Labor
   matters (such as family
   medical leave)
Internal Revenue Service/
   tax issues
Workers' compensation/
   unemployment benefits

Even as these issue areas and tasks were being distributed, Rebecca knew that some turnover of personnel could be expected and that shifts might occur with respect to the division of labor across the staff. Still, she felt that progress was being made and that things were at least beginning to fall into place.

During this period of transition, the Battle Creek office became a source of concern. First, there was displeasure in that quarter over the constituent service areas that had been assigned. Not only was the staff there a bit unhappy that they had not been given one of the substantive issue areas they had wanted, but they also believed that the areas they had been assigned (veterans' issues and Social Security) were more labor-intensive than those given to the other offices. Moreover, Rebecca and Danielle Moreland did not get off to a very good start. Apparently, Danielle had expected to be named district director, and before any of the staff appointments were announced, she had begun introducing herself as such. Rebecca noted, "This caused a fair amount of confusion. When I first started putting things together, it was rather awkward, to say the least, to explain to people that 'Danielle works for me; no, she is not the district director.' Frankly, most of us wondered from the start if things could work out between the two of us, given that she wasn't much of a team player."

There were other indications of trouble early on in the Battle Creek office. The office seemed to be left unattended too frequently—calls were going into voice mail often, and both Danielles seemed to be spending a great deal of time outside the office. Additionally, word got back to Rebecca that Danielle Moreland was saying inappropriate things about the congressman and that, at times, her attitude was somewhat haughty and even belligerent. The situation reached a boiling point when Moreland overstepped her authority on an issue involving the rights of a prisoner in one of Michigan's state prisons. When a person was incarcerated, he or she was asked about religious or spiritual needs. The prison system then saw to it that those stated needs were met in as reasonable a fashion as possible. A prisoner, however, was allowed to make such a declaration only once a year, since inmates had become rather savvy about claiming to be Jewish on Friday nights and Saturday, as well as on the major Jewish holidays, then becoming Christian on Sundays and at Easter and Christmas, suddenly professing to be Muslim during Ramadan, and so forth.

Danielle Moreland was drawn into a situation involving a Native American who first declared his desire to practice his native religion, and then, sometime later in the same year, decided that he wanted to profess Christianity. Given the rules, the latter request was denied, and the prisoner contacted the Schwarz office in Battle Creek for redress. In recounting the episode, Rebecca observed that Danielle was a very religious person, and also part Native American. "The matter really hit home for her and she felt very passionate about it. To her, it was unbelievable that a person could not have a crucifix or any of the other objects associated with Christianity if they wanted them." In her zeal, however, Danielle threatened the legislative liaison to the State Department of Corrections with a congressional investigation if this prisoner's religious requests were not accommodated. She also intimated that she could have the Department of Corrections deluged with an email protest campaign from

Michigan's considerable Native American population. As it happened, the legislative liaison was a personal friend of both John Truscott and Rebecca. When she learned of Danielle's threat, Rebecca knew that it was time to take action.

Rebecca called Danielle Moreland and told her that she was off the case and was to make no more calls related to it. "She had crossed the line," Rebecca said. "We just don't advocate for constituents in that combative way. My goodness, we won't do that for our strongest supporters; why on earth would we do that in this situation?" During the same week that the prisoner incident came to a head, Rebecca received calls from three different people who told her that the staff in Battle Creek was unprofessional and disrespectful. At that point, Rebecca called Matt Marsden to tell him that the situation in Battle Creek office had become untenable. Matt agreed that both Danielle Moreland and Danielle Miller had to go.

Matt went to the Human Resources office on Capitol Hill for advice about removing these employees, and that office agreed that termination was appropriate. Typically, Matt was told, employees are given the option of signing a letter of resignation or getting a letter of dismissal. (Each eventually chose the former.) Both Rebecca and Matt were saddened that things had not worked out in the Battle Creek office. Rebecca felt particularly badly about Danielle Miller, who, in her opinion, "had simply chosen the wrong role model to follow."

Battle Creek had to be re-staffed quickly, and so Paul Egnatuk agreed to take over the operation there. In April he hired Jeremy Whittum, who had been a township supervisor in Eaton County and had a feel for constituent work. Dawn Saylor, who had interned in the office during her senior year at Albion College, was hired after she graduated in the spring.

Paul's move to the Battle Creek office left a hole in the staffing arrangement in Delta Township, making it possible for Matt to bring in another person there—an idea he had been toying with for some time. Since Matt was frequently in Washington, and Paul and Cheryl were often out of the office on constituent business or in meetings, Faye was left alone, save for a college intern, a great deal of the time. Matt was concerned about security issues in the Delta office—if, for instance, a disgruntled constituent were to show up looking to cause trouble. Matt also believed that it would be helpful to bring in someone who could serve as his "stand-in" while he was away. Finally, it was clear that Faye was being pulled in too many directions. She was trying to keep the long-term calendar in order, but she was finding that management of the demands of the daily calendar precluded her putting into effect a well-organized long-term plan for scheduling the congressman's time. Matt thought it would be a good idea to have someone else to keep the daily calendar as well as to provide backup in the Delta office.

Even before Paul moved to Battle Creek, Matt had contacted an old friend to see if he was interested in joining the Schwarz staff. John Berg had been a fraternity brother at Michigan State and, like Matt, had worked in the governor's office. After leaving that position, John went to work as a contract employee doing computer and database management for General Motors. After five years in that position—during which time he had been unable to move to a permanent place in the GM workforce—he was growing concerned about being let go without warning and about the health of the company as well, so when Matt wanted to talk about his working for Congressman Schwarz, John was ready to listen. When the decision was made to have Paul Egnatuk leave Delta Township for Battle Creek, Matt made it clear to Rebecca that they needed someone in the Delta office to serve as his eyes and ears when he was in D.C., as well as to help Faye with scheduling. Matt clearly trusted John, and because he had spent time in the governor's office, John understood political operations. John summed up his hiring in simple terms: "Matt said to me, 'Look I could really use someone in Delta, you've done this sort of work before, it would bring you back into politics, and your joining us would be very helpful to me and to the whole Schwarz operation.' So...here I am."

It was understood that John would be placed under Rebecca on the organizational chart of the Schwarz staff, but that most of his interaction would be directly with Matt. Initially, John was given the task of handling the congressman's daily schedule, being told of any changes to the day by staffers in Washington when Schwarz was in D.C. and staying in regular contact with Rebecca or Matt when Joe was in the district. Room changes, time changes, and any other alterations to the daily schedule came through John, who would make certain to put the changes out on e-mail

In the Delta offices, John Berg (above left) took on the responsibilities of scheduling, assisting Matt Marsden in D.C., and coordinating service academy nominations, while Cheryl Nebbeling (above right), who took over for Cheryl Chapko, focused on immigration issues. In the Battle Creek office, Jeremy Whittum (left) handled issues involving veterans and military affairs.

and text message so that they were immediately available to anyone who needed to know where the congressman was at any given moment.

John picked up a couple of other responsibilities when he arrived in Delta Township. He was to make sure, for example, that the interns were doing the daily clippings—a typical congressional office task. Some member of the staff is given the responsibility of carefully combing through the district's newspapers. All print pieces that refer to the congressman are clipped, summarized, and filed, and any articles on major policy issues affecting the district are catalogued as a way to help the legislator keep tabs on public sentiment in the constituency. Some congressional offices also clip articles about major accomplishments from the local papers so that the office can generate a letter of congratulations to the press-worthy constituent—signed, of course, by the member of

Congress. John estimated that this task of clipping, summarizing, and filing could take between two and four hours a day, and he was glad that it could be regularly handed off to a college intern.

One of the more interesting responsibilities that John took on after he arrived in Delta was coordinating the congressman's nominations to the U.S. service academies. Each member of Congress can nominate a total of ten students each year to the Naval Academy at Annapolis, Maryland, the Military Academy at West Point, New York, the Air Force Academy at Colorado Springs, Colorado, and the Merchant Marine Academy at Kings Point, New York. No applicant can be accepted for study at any of the academies without a letter of recommendation from his or her member of the House of Representatives, from one of his or her senators, or from the vice president of the United States. Legislators take this process quite seriously.

John put together a small group of people to review requests for these letters of recommendation. The group included a navy physician, a couple of constituents with extensive military backgrounds, and a couple of staff members with international experience. (Because service academy graduates are quite likely to be sent overseas, John thought that people with international experience would bring a helpful viewpoint to the decision process.) Twelve requests had been made between January and the fall of 2005, and eight of them made it to every group member's list as worthy of serious consideration. A day was set aside during the week before Thanksgiving for each of the candidates to meet with John's group in the Jackson district office conference room.

Having attended a congressional workshop on the process earlier in the fall, John had learned more than he probably cared to about the admissions process to the U.S. service academies. In that workshop, he was particularly struck by a presentation given by a military physician, who went through a list of health problems that virtually disqualified candidates. "Frankly, it seemed kind of cold," John recalled. "This doctor said, 'Hey, if someone has asthma, rheumatoid arthritis, and/or one of several other conditions, don't bother writing for them because they're not going to get in.'" Nonetheless, John was impressed with what he learned about the academies and the education they provide. "These potential students are fighting for a great opportunity," he observed. In the end, Congressman Schwarz wrote letters of recommendation for seven applicants.

Another task that Berg took on was, as he labeled it, "postal service issues"—a more complicated area than one might imagine. On more than one occasion, John found himself in an uncomfortable position between a constituent who wanted help and the U.S. Postal Service, which was not eager to provide relief. John observed with some surprise in his voice, that

> the postal service is a very tight organization, and if they don't want you to have a mailbox on or beside your door, they will make you go through all kinds of hoops to convince them that it's necessary. We had a young guy, who lived in the Jackson area, with a lung condition that is exacerbated by cold air. His mailbox is down by the curb near the end of his driveway, and on cold days it's really tough on him to walk down and get his mail. So we made a request that he be permitted to have a mail drop at his front door so that in the winter he could just reach out to get his mail. The response from the postal people was clear and definitive. They said, "There's no way in hell we're moving his postal drop from the curb to his door. Our carrier reports that this guy is always out front cutting his own lawn. Don't tell us he can cut his lawn but not get his mail."

Even after being assured that the man's condition was affected by climate changes, the postal service was unmoved, and John's request was denied.

Each member of the congressman's staff could tell a story about a strange set of circumstances that arose in his or her particular constituent service area. Dawn Saylor, for example, who handled a wide variety of Social Security issues, found that nothing in her political science studies at Albion College had prepared her for some of the situations and characters she encountered while working out of the Battle Creek office. One case that she claimed she would never understand involved a young man who had been denied Social Security benefits and was being evicted from his home. When the constituent provided a copy of the foreclosure notice on his house, Dawn did everything she could do to expedite an appeal hearing on the denial of benefits. The denial was upheld on appeal, however. After the process had run its course, Dawn learned that the constituent had all along had access to a significant amount of money in a trust fund, so he hadn't had a legitimate Social Security claim after all. When Dawn asked him why he hadn't reported the trust fund, he explained that he was fighting with his parents, who had set up the fund for him, and he had not wanted to give them the satisfaction of using the money. The case left Dawn shaking her head. "That's just so odd," she observed. "It's totally beyond me."

Some other constituent requests came on the heels of truly tragic circumstances, while still others were just plain funny. One situation that particularly touched Dawn involved a woman with an inoperable brain tumor who suffered numerous seizures on a daily basis. "One day," Dawn recounted,

> this woman's husband took off and left her and three children. The next day she received a letter from the Social Security Administration, informing her that her claim for Social Security disability was denied. And…it gets worse. Not long after the disability claim was denied, she was holding her youngest child, an infant, and she had a seizure. She dropped the baby, and the baby suffered brain damage. Social Services came in and took her kids away, claiming she was an unfit mother. There were times when I was on the phone with her that I just couldn't hold back the tears.

Dawn was able to help this woman by expediting the appeals process on the denial of disability. Ultimately, the appeal was resolved in the constituent's favor, and the woman did get some financial relief. Being able to help a constituent in need brought Dawn a great deal of satisfaction.

Not all of her work in constituent services proved so satisfying, however. Dawn admitted that when she started her job, she had thought, as she put it, "that some people were simply not in the mood to work and were just looking for a way to scam the system." People like the woman with the brain tumor helped to temper some of that cynicism, but other individuals reinforced her initial view. One such freeloader was a man who had been in phone contact with the office, claiming that he needed disability benefits because he had back problems. "The Michigan caseload was backlogged, and some of the cases were being shipped to Social

Security offices in other states. This guy's case was sent to California, and I was able to get his hearing expedited," Dawn explained.

I had noticed that everything coming out of California seemed to approve payments, and indeed, this fellow eventually received word that he was going to get his disability benefits. He came into the office to meet with us and to say thank you. I was startled when I saw him...it's obvious that he works out. In fact, it looks like he spends all day in the gym. There was no record of mental or emotional problems in his case file, just back problems. I couldn't help wondering just how severe the back problems are, given how fit the guy looks. He was so thankful that we had gotten him his Social Security money that, as he was leaving, he said to me, "If you ever need anybody's butt kicked, call me. I'll be glad to do it for you."

Ruefully, Dawn concluded that "the work can be exasperating, but that's true of any work, I guess."

Dawn also commented that, in some situations, she was just astounded with what some people would call in to say. "One quite elderly woman came in...she honestly wanted the congressman to introduce a bill that would prevent anybody who came from the Middle East from being a pharmacist. She was convinced that any Middle Easterner who was a pharmacist was going to poison her." In many ways, much of the work that occupied Dawn's time underscored just how far Battle Creek is from the majestic halls of Capitol Hill.

Congressional staffing is characterized by a great deal of turnover. Sometimes, while working in the office of a member of Congress, staffers make contacts that lead to job offers that are too good to pass up. In other cases, the pace of the work and the emotional toll that it can take lead staffers to seek less stressful employment elsewhere. In late summer of 2005, Rebecca's friend Cheryl Chapko, who had been working in the Delta office, left to take a position with a Lansing-based lobbying firm. Chapko had been very helpful to Rebecca in setting up the offices, and she had also worked on immigration issues. To replace her, Rebecca hired Cheryl Nebbeling, insisting with a laugh that the hiring decision was not predicated on saving the rest of the staff the work of learning a new name.

Joe Schwarz's District Staff

District Office	Name	Office Tasks and Legislative Policy Areas
Jackson	**Rebecca Schneider** *district director*	Setup and supervision of all three district offices and their staffs
	Rob Glazier *agriculture expert*	Agricultural policy and programs, outreach to farming community, immigration casework
	Jeane Johnson *outreach coordinator*	Contact groups in district (particularly senior citizens)
	Deanna Wiltse *office assistant*	Clerical work, answer phones, greet visitors, gatekeeper
Delta Township	**Paul Egnatuk** *office manager* (later moved to Battle Creek)	Local government and business liaison
	Faye Armstrong *executive assistant*	Coordinating congressman's long-term schedule
	Cheryl Chapko *constituent relations* *representative* (later left to join lobbying firm)	Medicare, IRS
	Cheryl Nebbeling *constituent relations* *representative* (replaced Chapko)	Immigration issues
	John Berg *constituent relations* *representative*	Daily and 2-week calendar scheduling, assisting Marsden, supervision of interns, coordinating service academy nominations, postal service issues

Joe Schwarz's District Staff (continued)

District Office	Name	Office Tasks and Legislative Policy Areas
Battle Creek	**Danielle Moreland** *constituent relations* *representative* (resigned)	Veterans issues, matters related to current military personnel
	Danielle Miller *constituent relations* *representative* (resigned)	Social Security
	Paul Egnatuk *office manager* (moved from Delta office)	
	Jeremy Whittum *constituent relations* *representative* (replaced Moreland)	Veterans and military affairs
	Dawn Saylor *constituent relations* *representative* (replaced Miller)	Social Security

"Two Cheryls, two Danielles...it did keep things interesting, if not a bit confusing," Rebecca acknowledged.

Rebecca wanted a "people person, someone who was approachable, a friendly face with really good people skills." In her opinion, Nebbeling, who lived in Delta Township and had done some coursework at the local community college, was the right person for the job. Cheryl took over the immigration issue area and found the work very satisfying. She was gratified, for example, by her role in facilitating the processing of paperwork that was necessary for a nun from Mexico to be granted U.S. citizenship. Like every congressional staffer, however, Cheryl got her share of peculiar requests. Rebecca sent one case to Nebbeling that left both women shaking their heads. A constituent had called Rebecca with what he claimed was a major problem. He explained that he intended to leave Detroit that evening for England in order to take his family to the Wimbledon Tennis Championships, and he had just learned that one of his sons did not have a passport. It was 9:00 a.m.—he wanted the Schwarz office to help him get a passport issued and delivered in twelve hours.

After a couple of phone calls, Cheryl determined that it could be done. The passport processing facility in Miami could issue the passport if the application made it there by late morning. The Wimbledon-bound constituent hired a courier to fly down to Miami from Detroit with all of the application material, wait while the passport was processed and drawn up, and then fly back to Detroit with the document. The passport was on a Detroit-bound plane by 2:00 p.m. and the family was off to enjoy the traditional strawberries and cream at Wimbledon. As Rebecca put it, "One would think that if this guy was going to invest $20,000 in a family vacation, he would have thought to check that everyone's travel papers were in order. Of course, if you can afford to vacation like that, the cost of sending a person to Florida to pick up a passport in one day probably isn't an issue."

Being able to produce a passport so quickly for a constituent was an accomplishment, but, as Rebecca noted, this kind of success is not entirely positive. "The natural reaction is to think, 'Wow, that's a really effective congressional office.' But, it's both a blessing and a curse. In the end," she continued, "you've enabled those people to repeat their behavior. They'll expect it next time. Cheryl did great work on something that never should have happened."

While Cheryl Nebbeling was dealing with immigration and citizenship issues in Delta, Rob Glazier was busy working with the agricultural community out of the Jackson office. Rob estimated that he received twenty-five to thirty calls a month from constituents with varied needs. "The most common activity I engaged in was outreach," Rob explained. He was often on the agenda at monthly meetings of professional associations such as the Farm Bureau or the Grange in various parts of the district. Rob's function at these meetings was to explain any changes in agricultural policy or to note the availability of new programs for those who work in the agricultural sector.

During his time in the Jackson office, Rob was able to let some farmers know what they could do to qualify for cash payments from the Department of Agriculture for operating environmentally friendly farms. This is the kind of constituent work that really allows a congressional office to serve as an important nexus between the people and the federal government, making constituents aware that their needs are being monitored and met. Rob was responsible for many other tasks as well. In one instance, a new ethanol production plant was scheduled for a grand opening and ribbon-cutting ceremony that Congressman Schwarz was to participate in. In preparing for the plant-opening ceremonies, it came to Rob's attention that the Alcohol, Tobacco, and Firearms (ATF) permits typically issued to plants working with explosive chemicals or fuels were not all in place. A hurried round of phone calls and faxes between Rob, ATF administrators, and field inspectors produced the proper permissions, and the ribbon-cutting came off without a hitch.

Without a doubt, a different focus characterizes the congressional offices in the district than that which is evident in a representative's office on Capitol Hill. In fact, the district offices sometimes appear to be a parallel world, working for the congressman yet seldom seeing him. District staffers are busy with a variety of "outside the Beltway" constituent matters, while the D.C. staff is caught up in the work that accompanies the boss's committee assignments and daily legislative routine. Nevertheless, all staff members—whether toiling in the heart of Michigan's Seventh District or in Room 128 of the Cannon Building on Independence Avenue—had to remember Chuck Yessaian's admonition on the day before Congressman Schwarz was sworn in: "At the end of the day, it's all about constituents."

7

Playing the Policy Game
It Could Be a Matter of Life or Death

A CONGRESSMAN, REPRESENTATIVE Schwarz learned early on, can be asked to address issues that raise profound moral questions as well as to deal with bread-and-butter issues that are critical to the folks in the district. In March 2005, just three months after Swearing-In Day, the national press went into a feeding frenzy over the fate of a forty-one-year-old Florida woman who had been in what court-appointed doctors called a "persistent vegetative state" since her heart stopped suddenly in February 1990. Terri Schiavo had collapsed in the hallway of the apartment she shared with her husband Michael. Paramedics who responded to her husband's 911 call found her face down, not breathing, with no pulse. Terri was defibrillated several times and then taken to the hospital. She had suffered both cardiac and respiratory arrest, and because of the length of time that her brain was not receiving oxygen, parts of the brain that allow for cognition, awareness, and perception had been damaged. Physicians could not agree on whether her condition was absolutely irreversible, and for years she was kept alive by nutrition and hydration delivered through a feeding tube.

Legal battles ensued between Michael Schiavo, who claimed that Terri would not have wanted to be kept alive in the condition she was in, and her parents, who contended that because of Terri's strict adherence to the tenets of Roman Catholicism, she never would have consented to removal of the feeding tube. A 2001 decision in the state courts of Florida allowing the feeding tube to be removed was followed by the passage of "Terri's law" in the Florida state legislature. This measure allowed Florida

Governor Jeb Bush to intervene in the matter, and the governor ordered that the feeding tube be reinserted. Terri's law was subsequently declared unconstitutional, and Governor Bush's attempt to have the case heard by the U.S. Supreme Court failed. The Florida judge who had originally allowed the removal of the feeding tube set March 18, 2005, as the date on which it could be permanently removed.

Congress became involved in the matter during the week of March 14, when the Senate passed a bill calling for federal court jurisdiction in the Schiavo case. The Republican leadership in the House called members back for an unusual Sunday night session on Palm Sunday, March 20, to consider the Senate legislation. The bill passed the House on a vote of 302–58 at 12:42 a.m. on Monday, March 21, and was signed into law by President Bush at 1:11 a.m. Even after the procedural assistance extended to their side by the congressional action, however, lawyers for Terri's parents, Mary and Bob Schindler, failed to win a ruling in federal court that would have allowed the feeding tube to be reinserted. By March 26, they appeared to have run out of legal options, and Terri Schiavo died on the morning of March 31, 2005.

Congressman Schwarz was unhappy that Congress had gotten involved in the Schiavo case. When asked how he had approached the issue, he said quickly, "I dealt with it as a physician." His voice was tinged with frustration as he recounted the episode: "I got a message on the BlackBerry, and I just knew they were going to force me to come back on Sunday night and vote on an issue that I believed we shouldn't be voting on. But I was not going to run away from it." Schwarz continued, "In general, some of the pressing end-of-life issues might rise to the level of some sort of congressional hearing or investigation, but not on the basis of a single situation at a particular point in time."

In a discussion of the Schiavo matter, the congressman was blunt in his criticism of the House leadership:

> This issue was before us because some of our most zealous members, particularly Mr. DeLay [then majority leader in the House] wanted to make a public display on something that they could define as a right-to-life issue. To say that this was not being done because some in our party were look-

ing to gain politically would raise disingenuousness to an art form. . . . I would not have chosen to vote on it, and I suspect that three or four other physicians in the Congress would say the same thing. But there it was and as a physician, I saw no other way to vote. This person had robust brain-stem activity, spontaneous respiration, spontaneous cardiac activity, was in no imminent danger of dying, she wasn't on life support, not on a respirator, and she was being given nourishment through a feeding tube... along with at least 15,000 other people in this country who at one level or another have decreased clinical abilities. So, what do we do now? Take the feeding tubes out of all 15,000? I don't think so.

Congressman Schwarz voted with his party, but he certainly was not pleased with how his Republican colleagues had framed the question and brought the Terri Schiavo case to the floor of the House.

The Schiavo episode lingered in the minds of the public for quite some time, and Congressman Schwarz remained steadfast in his criticism of how his party had handled the issue. In October, when he participated on a panel with a professor of critical care medicine and a vicar at a symposium on critical care sponsored by the Battle Creek Health System, Representative Schwarz's comments on the Schiavo case were forceful and direct: "I thought then, and still feel today, that it is not the business of Congress to become involved in these decisions. It was former Majority Leader Tom DeLay who called representatives back to Washington to vote on the matter. He made a mistake by asking Congress to come back. There is a very strong feeling that these discussions should take place in the state legislature."

On another issue of "life and death" magnitude, Congressman Schwarz was completely engaged. In the summer of 2004, President Bush announced that limited federal funding would be allowed for embryonic stem-cell research, but only on available stem-cell lines derived from embryos that had already been discarded. Proponents of more comprehensive research programs found this ruling too restrictive; they had hoped for funding for the use of frozen cells stored in fertility clinics after it was determined that the cells were not going to be used for in vitro fertilization.

The issue of stem-cell research had inspired vigorous debate in recent years, fueled in part by the active support of prominent advocates such as Nancy Reagan, who spoke out on the promise of research efforts in the treatment of Alzheimer's, the devastating disease that afflicted former president Ronald Reagan, and actor Christopher Reeve, who worked tirelessly to increase funding for stem-cell research in the hope that it would someday help people like himself who had suffered spinal cord injuries. Although it was passionately opposed in the fundamentalist religious community—where such experimentation was viewed as akin to abortion—embryonic stem-cell research had broad support in the scientific community. Most political liberals and moderates also favored such research, and the cause was taken up vigorously by the Tuesday Group, an organization of moderate Republican members of Congress.

On February 15, 2005, Congressman Michael Castle of Delaware, who was both a member of the Tuesday Group and the president of the Main Street Partnership (as noted in chapter 2, a larger group with centrist values), introduced H.R. 810, a bill calling for extending federal funding to include research on new stem-cell lines. The Stem Cell Research Enhancement Act of 2005 sought to provide funding for the use of cells derived from embryos that were going to be discarded by fertility clinics. Typically, the in vitro fertilization procedure involves retrieval of enough cell samples for multiple pregnancies; once a couple decides that they do not want any more children, the excess or surplus matter is discarded as medical waste. Castle's bill was designed to reclaim this surplus material for research purposes. Calling for donor consent to use of the embryos for medical research and for strict regulation by the Department of Health and Human Services, the bill quickly garnered 200 cosponsors, representing an impressive display of bipartisan support.

Still, the proponents of H.R. 810 knew that they were fighting an uphill battle. President Bush had vowed publicly to veto any effort by Congress to increase the federal government's role in stem-cell research. Moreover, the right wing of the Republican Party in Congress, led by Majority Leader DeLay, was vehemently opposed to any such legislation and hoped to prevent this bill, or anything like it, from coming to the House floor for a vote.

On March 1, 2005, two weeks after H.R. 810 was introduced, it was the principal topic on the agenda at the Tuesday Group's Wednesday meeting. There was much to discuss. The bill had been sent to the House Committee on Energy and Commerce, but its supporters were concerned that the measure might never get to the House floor. Moreover, a drama was playing out that served to raise the ire of the bill's opponents. It became known that the Main Street Partnership had commissioned a public opinion poll in thirteen congressional districts, conducted by the same polling organization that usually worked for the Bush White House, and that the poll results were overwhelmingly supportive of an increased federal role in stem-cell research. Indeed, one of the districts included in the poll sample was that of an outspoken critic of H.R. 810, who reacted furiously to the news that the poll had been done.

"The guy is a hothead," Congressman Schwarz reported, "and he just went off...bonkers." As Joe's account of the episode reveals, this legislator's antagonism eventually breached the decorum of the House:

> He physically threatened Mark Kirk [R-Ill.], a bill cosponsor and ardent supporter of embryonic stem-cell research. Kirk was talking with some others down on the House floor about the bill, and this fellow just bursts out at Kirk, "That's bullshit...you little son of a bitch...." So, Kirk puts up his hand and says, "Let's just calm down and have a civil conversation here." And the other guy says, "Get your hands off me, you little son of a bitch," and starts pushing Kirk. Two other congressmen had to get between them because this guy seemed to genuinely want to fight with Mark, and frankly, that's just dumb. Kirk is not a big guy, but he was trained as a fighter pilot who saw service in both Kosovo and Iraq. He also served in navy intelligence. You don't want to fight with him...that's not smart. Not that it's ever smart to get in a fistfight. I know that was not uncommon in the nineteenth-century Congress, but come on....

In an attempt to restore civility, Representatives Castle and Kirk asked Speaker of the House Dennis Hastert to meet with them and a couple of the members who had been angered by the poll. Castle reported on the meeting to the Tuesday Group at lunch: "I just said, 'Look. Mark and I are very sorry...we know that you were offended if your district was polled without your knowing it. But you have to understand, it was not our poll and we certainly did not pick the districts.'" The Tuesday Group, however, knew that emotions were running high with respect to H.R. 810.

Supporters of the legislation firmly believed that if they failed to demonstrate how seriously invested in the bill they were, it would never get a floor vote. They therefore adopted a proactive strategy that essentially called for threatening the Speaker of the House. Representative Castle drafted a letter, signed by several members of the Tuesday Group, to make it clear that if H.R. 810 were not given an up-or-down vote, they would not vote with the Republican leadership in support of President Bush's budget. When the Speaker learned of the existence of this letter, which had not yet been sent, he allowed a group of about ten moderates, including Congressman Schwarz, to meet with him to discuss bringing the bill to the floor. The Speaker was told that the letter would not be sent or released to the press if H.R. 810 got a floor vote.

Describing the discussion with Hastert as "a very modulated, productive meeting," Congressman Schwarz continued, "The Speaker is a superb listener, and he listened intently to everything we had to say. He asked appropriate questions, and he said he'd let us know within twenty-four hours if we could get our up-or-down vote. I think the Speaker is a fairly moderate fellow, and he's certainly a bright fellow. But in his position he has to deal with those who are less moderate, more inflammatory and visceral in their reaction to these kinds of issues."

In the meeting, Schwarz spoke last—and he spoke longer than anyone else.

> If people are opposed to stem-cell research on some religious or moral basis, fine. I would not try to sway a person from the rock of their beliefs, whatever they may be. But do not impugn people like those in our group, or every Democrat in the House of Representatives, and every expert in the finest universities who will tell you, chapter and verse, from peer-reviewed publications, that embryonic stem-cell research can provide powerful findings that will lead to treatments of some very tragic diseases. I won't argue with anyone who steps up and says I have religious issues here…it's not my place or anyone else's to pass judgment on the religious beliefs of others. But don't argue the science with me. If you argue the science with me, you are dead wrong.

Congressman Schwarz reported that his goal in presenting his views was to explain to Speaker Hastert, as plainly as possible, what he viewed as the logic behind H.R. 810 and the science behind that logic.

Joe Schwarz is a practical guy, and there was another dimension to the debate that he was quick to point out. He was convinced that if the United States did not support embryonic stem-cell research, much would be lost to other countries in terms of grant money, scientific expertise, and a host of other business-related benefits. "If you look at this from a cold, hard business point of view, there is no way you can afford to pass on this kind of research," Schwarz contended.

The day after the meeting with Hastert, word got out that the Speaker would agree to bring H.R. 810 to the floor. Joe was approached by the House Republican Conference chair,[1] Deborah Pryce, who told him, "The Speaker is giving you this vote because of your presentation, Joe." "Thank you very much," Schwarz responded. "I'm glad it worked out well because we need this vote." It would be a couple of months before action was taken, but H.R. 810 passed the House on May 24, 2005, by a vote of 238–194. That week, the *Kalamazoo Gazette* praised Schwarz for his commonsense behavior, declaring, "It makes little sense for embryos to be thrown out...when they offer researchers an important opportunity to discover life-saving therapies for people with a wide range of illnesses."[2] In July of 2006, the bill passed the Senate and was sent to the president.

Public policy is often the result of collaborative efforts by informal work groups comprised of people with similar policy interests. Meetings with like-minded colleagues are a staple of the congressional scene. One such group is the Michigan Republican House delegation, which tries to meet early every Wednesday morning when the House is in session to discuss legislative strategies, pitch ideas or bills to one another, seek cosponsors for proposed legislation, and share information. The location of the meeting rotates among the members' offices, and the host typically has the House catering service bring in coffee, juice, sweet rolls, and bagels. Sometimes, the group invites a guest to join them.

On March 2, 2005, Congressman Schwarz hosted a meeting of the Michigan Republican delegation, to which the new secretary of commerce, Carlos Gutierrez, was invited to talk about trade policy. Gutierrez had been chairman of the board of the Kellogg Company when he was appointed by President Bush to head the Commerce Department. Born in Havana, Cuba, Gutierrez had come to the United States with his family at the age of seven, joined Kellogg as a sales representative when he was twenty-three, and at forty-six had become president and chief executive officer—the youngest in the company's history. Because Gutierrez had spent so many years at Kellogg, the largest company in Congressman Schwarz's hometown of Battle Creek, the two knew each other well.

Five of Michigan's eight Republican House members attended this particular Wednesday meeting. As they arrived and got coffee, they exchanged friendly hellos and introduced themselves to Secretary Gutierrez, sometimes with a bit of the posturing that makes watching Washington politics such a popular spectator sport. Rep. Vern Ehlers, from the Michigan Third District, and chair of the Subcommittee on Environment, Technology, and Standards of the House Committee on Science, for example, offered his hand and said, "Nice to meet you, Mr. Secretary. I have jurisdiction over 70 percent of your budget." The group soon got down to business.

There was a great deal of give-and-take during the frank exchange about trade policies. Secretary Gutierrez was there to garner support for the Central America Free Trade Agreement (CAFTA) that was being pursued by the Bush administration. He was met with friendly combativeness by the congressmen in attendance, who were more interested in discussing enforcement of existing trade arrangements. One said, "Hey, your administration's failure to enforce trade laws is killing us. The amount of counterfeiting of goods that goes on in China is just killing U.S. manufacturers." The secretary responded with a rueful smile, "I know all about that. … One of the most popular counterfeit items for sale on a worldwide basis is a box of Kellogg's Frosted Flakes. I believe I have a pretty good sense of the counterfeiting problem."

Congressman Mike Rogers, however, could not hide the frustration in his voice as he responded to the secretary's push for support on CAFTA: "I have supported every trade agreement that this administration has sponsored, and I am just afraid that we are not getting enforcement from the White House. We go out and cheerlead for these policies, and then we get killed back home…as these arrangements end up costing us jobs by sending them out of the country." Registering the group's tone of mild resistance, Gutierrez indicated that he was preparing for a round of trade meetings with Canada and Mexico, and he promised to meet with the group again before Thanksgiving—which was to say sometime within the next eight months. The meeting adjourned, and the secretary headed for his office downtown, a considerable institutional distance from the Cannon House Office Building.

Life on Capitol Hill, however, is not only about dramatic votes and presidential bill signings in the middle of the night, or fighting for legislation that members feel passionately about, or meetings with cabinet secretaries to debate trade policy. Even as the congressman was finding his way in the heart of the legislative arena, his staff was learning about the institution's more mundane underbelly.

Meghan Kolassa, the young attorney on Joe's staff, spent significant time during her first year on the Hill dealing with a rather unusual facility problem. In late January 2005, as the congressman's personal effects arrived in D.C., the staff realized that Joe's office could not accommodate all of the framed artwork that had been brought along. They decided to hang some of the pictures in the room that housed the legislative assistants—the room, as Meghan laughingly explained, "where all the magic happens. Really, we're like the elves in Santa's workshop…doing all the work behind the scenes." Meghan selected two pieces of artwork to hang on either side of the large window at the back of the room.

Shortly after the pieces were hung, however, she began to notice an unpleasant, musty smell—"that dirty, stinky smell of socks that have been left in a gym locker for too long"—near her desk, which was located less than two feet from one of the pictures. Having played water polo in college, Meghan was well acquainted with locker room scents, so, she recounted,

> …I spent a week or more trying to isolate the smell. Finally, I had to lean over for a piece of paper that I had dropped, and my nose got close to the wall, and I pulled back suddenly, saying loudly to no one in particular, "Wow, man, this is gross." So I moved the painting, and something was growing on the wall and had gotten on the brown paper backing of this

Meghan Kolassa (above left), legislative assistant, Chuck Yessaian (above right), legislative director, and Jared Page (right), legislative assistant, go about the daily business of running the D.C. operation—mold or no mold.

framed piece. And my mind starts racing...oh great! This is going to turn into some huge thing, and I'm going to have to buy or repair this thing. Luckily it didn't eat too far into the paper.

Thus began the saga of "Meghan's Mold." At Chuck's suggestion, she called the housekeeping department in the House of Representatives, telling them, "I've got a big furry patch growing on my wall and it's gross."

That office connected her to the folks in the maintenance department, which made Meghan a little nervous—"I had fears of someone slapping paint on the wall and proclaiming the problem solved. Meanwhile, my nose was starting to itch and I seemed to be getting headaches everyday."

No quick response was forthcoming from any of the House maintenance or painting staff, until, finally, one night after the Cannon Office Building had closed, the maintenance people came in and bleached the dinner-plate-sized spot on the wall, and then chipped off the furry paint. Still, the odor remained. After a couple of weeks, Meghan called the maintenance department again to see if there was a plan for finishing the job. "So," she reported,

> …a guy comes over, says "Wow! We need to get some paint people out here." And now I start asking questions, like "Aren't we gonna figure out how this mold, or whatever it is, came about, rather than just shellacking back over it with paint?" You can imagine how relieved I was when he said, "Oh no, first we'll let the wall dry, then we'll put the clear stuff on so no moisture can come through, then we'll plaster and repaint. But before any of that happens we'll have to chip all the way down to the cement. Don't worry lady, this will all be taken care of . . . ."

After hearing this plan, Meghan said, she couldn't help but think of the old line, "Trust us, we're from the government."

When the crew from the painting department arrived some time later, they were unhappy that some members of the congressman's staff were working in the area. "Imagine," Meghan recounted with a sardonic laugh, "we wanted to work in our office during the day…how odd." After chipping away the top layer of the wall, the crew grew concerned about how wet the cement was. Meghan continued her story:

> The paint guy says, "I'm gonna have to come back in a day or two, or maybe I have to blow something on it, ya know, like a big fan, overnight. There's no way I can put sealant on it if it's wet." A couple of days later, there's a whole gaggle of guys looking at my wall, then going outside, and looking at it from outside the building. And they're checking things out, and they determine that the drainpipes that run all the way down the walls from the roof to the basement are leaking. Ultimately they say they are

going to find a temporary fix until they figure out what to do with the pipe situation.

The temporary fix was a coat of paint after the wall was reasonably dry.

The quick fix, not surprisingly, did not fix anything. As the spring rains came, the seepage became more pronounced—in fact, the wall changed colors. Because there were no pictures on the wall, however, there was no mold. (As it had been explained to Meghan, the backing of a piece of art allows a nice climate for mold to grow.) "Every time I called to see what the maintenance people were going to do about the wet walls," Meghan said, "everyone in the office laughed, because it was, in fact, getting sillier and sillier." Still, throughout the summer, she persevered, because nothing had been accomplished. Each time she called, she mentioned the mold problem, and each time the response was, "We see you've had some paint work done, but there's no record of any mold." Finally, Meghan was told that in August, when the House is in recess, the wall would be repaired. August and September came and went, but there was no activity on "Meghan's wall," as the congressman's staff referred to it.

When the fall rains came, the paint that remained on Meghan's wall began to develop little bubbles. "The guys in the office started calling it the alien wall," Meghan remembered, "telling me I had to be careful because an alien was about to come out of the wall." Meghan learned that there had been correspondence with a company that used some heating system to seal pipes in walls, but that company was unable to get clearance to work on the Hill. Sometime later, she became disgusted enough by the lack of progress that she began calling the Office of the Superintendent of the House of Representatives. No matter how many messages she left, however, the calls were never returned.

After more calls and more unanswered messages, suddenly Meghan thought she saw a way to force a solution:

> As it happened, the superintendent was in the building in late October for some function, or to look at something for the congressman while I happened to be in the congressman's office, and I just couldn't resist saying, "Hey, while you're over here, would you mind taking a look at my wall?" He said he would be glad to. When the superintendent looked at the mold,

his jaw dropped. "Oh my gosh. How long has this been going on?" When I briefed him, noting all the phone calls I had made, and the number of people who had been over to see it, he was absolutely stupefied. "I never heard anything about this. You are telling me that there was mold growing, the wall has been scraped down to the cement, plastered, shellacked, sealed, and repainted over the last ten months, and I knew nothing about it? That kind of work, in any of the House buildings should come through me." The superintendent told me, "I'll get this taken care of."

But as the calendar pages continued to turn, however, no action was taken.

The lawyer in Meghan believed that the House maintenance people would continue to call the problem a leakage issue and fail to acknowledge that a mold issue existed. "Legally," she observed, "they cannot afford to say that they have a mold problem, but now that someone is aware of it, I do believe that it will be taken care of, eventually. And I do get a smile out of the glamorous image that Congress has on CNN. To the average citizen, Congress is an ornate hearing room or the majestic Capitol dome seen in so many photos and movies. Congress is not about a year's worth of fur growing out of your wall."

While Meghan battled the mold and met her other, more policy-oriented responsibilities, Congressman Schwarz was acutely aware that the breezes of spring were not necessarily balmy in regard to the fortunes of some of his constituents. In late April, the *Kalamazoo Gazette* published a short piece about the efforts of Schwarz and his colleague Fred Upton to protect the military facilities located in Battle Creek. The Pentagon was awaiting a report from the Base Realignment and Closure Commission (BRAC)—made up of nine distinguished people, including former members of Congress, former cabinet officers, and retired high-ranking military personnel—which was to recommend a list of bases for closing or relocation. During the previous round of closures, in 1993, the Hart-Dole-Inouye Federal Center in Battle Creek had been targeted. Joe Schwarz, who was in the Michigan state senate at the time, had been instrumental in saving the center. Now he was again ready for battle. "Joe is like a bull in a china shop," observed Congressman Fred Upton, who also has constituents working at the center. "Joe is saying, 'Close a base in my district? Over my dead body!'"[3] Local television and radio also made mention of BRAC as the May 16, 2005, due date for the release of the commission's recommendations approached.

Congressman Schwarz and his staff prepared for the worst, while still trying to do everything they could to prevent closures in the district. There was a series of meetings with Senator Carl Levin (D-Mich.), the ranking member of the Senate Armed Services Committee, to discuss saving the federal center as well as the Battle Creek Air National Guard Base. Levin and Schwarz were on the same page when it came to the federal center, a facility with a fascinating history. It had begun as the Battle Creek Sanitarium, built by John Harvey Kellogg as a popular place for wealthy people to go on a health retreat. In 1942 the army bought the property for use as a hospital for convalescing soldiers—it was there that three future distinguished senators, Philip Hart (D-Mich.), Robert Dole (R-Kansas), and Daniel Inouye (D-Hawaii), met in the mid-1940s after suffering wounds in World War II battles overseas. Since the 1950s, the building had been used for military logistics. As Congressman Schwarz described the place, "It employs about 1,900 people, 98 percent of whom are DOD [Department of Defense] civilians with very high skill levels, essentially in computer operations. It's basically a cataloging operation. Every widget they have in the military, all branches, is inventoried there and they know where everything is." From Schwarz's perspective (which was shared by Levin), this was work that had to be done, and there was no point in undertaking a major relocation effort simply to have the same work done in a different place.

Aaron Taliaferro joined the Schwarz staff about three weeks before the BRAC list was to be released. Brought in as a senior legislative assistant because of his military background, he was acutely aware that if any recommended closures or relocations included facilities in Michigan's Seventh Congressional District, his job was to launch an all-out effort to get the recommendation reversed. One of the first things Aaron did, along with Chief of Staff Matt Marsden, was to contact the office of Rep. Candice Miller, whose Michigan district includes the Selfridge Air National Guard Base. But both of them were rebuffed by Miller's staff. "They're arrogant," Matt asserted. "They treated us like a know-nothing freshman office. They even told Aaron to back off and leave them alone. Oh well... we wanted to work together, collegially, to do all we could to save all of our interests. They didn't want to work with us, so I thought, 'Screw them, it's their loss.'"

When the BRAC recommendations were released, the Schwarz operation breathed a partial sigh of relief. The Seventh District's largest installation, the Hart-Dole-Inouye Federal Center, was not on the list. However, the Air National Guard Base, home to the 110th Fighter Wing, was recommended for closure. Aaron noted that Congressman Schwarz "evidenced some frustration, but never displayed any uncertainty. He rolled up his sleeves and simply said, 'We've got to save that base,' and that set the tone for me."

If any of the facilities in the Seventh District were going to appear on BRAC's list, Aaron said, the air base would be the easiest for him to deal with. "This was not hard for me to understand," he reported, "since I used to work for many of the folks who helped write the BRAC recommendation. The reason for our base ending up on the list was in the cost analysis, and I was trained as a military cost analyst." In previous realignment and closure decisions, local economic impact and job losses had been used in appealing such closures, but in 2005 the commission did not wish to hear arguments that were not related to cost savings or military value.

Aaron approached the task of reversing the recommendation methodically:

> I thought like a military analyst. First, identify the problem. OK, the problem is, we're on the list. The way to get off the list is quite straightforward. Invalidate the findings that resulted on our being on the closure list. How did they calculate the cost savings from closing us? And how did they calculate military value? So, I went to the volumes that had the commission's justifications in them, read through the reasoning, and set strategy to attack their findings. We also had some help from some fairly significant players.

According to Aaron, Lt. Col. Dave San Clemente, the operations officer on the base, was an "unsung hero" in the BRAC process. "He did a Herculean amount of data gathering and analysis for us," Aaron recounted, "and was absolutely essential to our work." San Clemente's efforts made up a large portion of the presentation to be made before the BRAC commission at a June meeting in St. Louis.

That meeting was an opportunity for Congressman Schwarz to make a public appeal for the Battle Creek base, and he brought along supporters to strengthen his case. An economic development group, Battle Creek Unlimited, played a key role in enlisting Dr. George Erickcek, a senior economist at the Upjohn Foundation, whose reputation for sound economic research made the questions raised about the commission's economic analysis seem less biased than if they had been raised by the Schwarz team. The chance to make their case to the commission, face-to-face, "was critical," Aaron said, "and set a very good tone."

The presentation was a success. Aaron took particular satisfaction from the comments made by one commissioner, Admiral Harold W. Gehman Jr., USN (Ret.), who singled out Michigan at a press conference at the conclusion of the day's hearings "for a very information-based, factual, logical, and coherent presentation." Many of the presentations from other states had focused on the economic impact of closures on local communities, and Aaron surmised from the commissioners' responses that those attempts to reverse the commission's recommendations had been less well received.

The final BRAC recommendation was expected in late August. In the time between the June meeting in St Louis and the final decision, Aaron met personally with eight of the nine commissioners. Setting up those meetings was not easy, but a friend of the Schwarz office, Nancy Barbour, a government relations expert with the law firm of Dykema Gossett, had a contact on the commission staff, and so she was able to arrange meetings with the commissioners. When Nancy managed to reserve a block of time for a meeting, she would alert Aaron, and he would try to have Congressman Schwarz, if possible, and one of the staff members from Senator Levin's office, if that could be arranged, join him in pressing the case for reversal. The goal of these meetings was to reinforce the message that had been delivered in St. Louis.

Aaron also used every contact he could to persuade Commissioner Sam Skinner to make a site visit to the Battle Creek Air National Guard Base. Skinner, who had been secretary of transportation and White

House chief of staff for President George H.W. Bush, also served in the U.S. Army Reserve and was a jet-certified pilot. The commissioner visited in late July, and as he toured the base, he noticed that Duncan Aviation was used for much of the aircraft maintenance. Recognizing Duncan as one of the premier aircraft maintenance companies in the United States, Skinner mused to Joe and Aaron, "...if we eliminate this base, we're removing from potential service to the Guard some of the best technicians in the world." Aaron gave a military-sounding response: "Yes, sir, that is correct." Both Joe and Aaron believed the site visit had gone well.

On Friday, August 26, 2005, the BRAC final report was released. To the delight of Congressman Schwarz and all who had worked with him on this issue, the initial recommendation to close the Air National Guard Base in Battle Creek was overturned. Schwarz was matter-of-fact in his public statement: "We secured meetings with BRAC commissioners and commission staff, and effectively conveyed our position that closing the air station does not increase the efficiency or effectiveness of our armed forces."

Newspaper editorials applauded Schwarz and his efforts to keep the base open. Laudatory pieces in the *Kalamazoo Gazette,* the *Battle Creek Enquirer,* the *Lansing State Journal,* as well as on most of the television newscasts in the district, uniformly cited the congressman for his aggressive battle to save the base. Schwarz's colleague Fred Upton was also effusive in his praise—the reversal of the decision to close the Battle Creek base, Upton claimed, was "a testament to the vigorous effort led by Joe Schwarz." George Weeks, writing in the *Detroit News,* said, "Good to see Joltin' Joe win a freshman victory by arguing military specifics, not just local economic issues that, for decades, were featured in base closure debates." [4]

Even as a freshman in the House of Representatives, Joe Schwarz had not been shy in standing up for what he believed. He was frank in stating his views about the Terri Schiavo matter, he actively supported legislation to advance stem-cell research, and he proved a capable advocate for Michigan's Seventh District in working to keep its endangered air base open. As he became more comfortable in his legislative role, he seemed well-positioned for reelection a year from November.

Reelection Politics

IT IS CONVENTIONAL wisdom that incumbent members of Congress have considerable advantages over challengers in an election campaign. Incumbents typically enjoy greater name recognition and easier access to the media. They also tend to have a wider network of contacts and donors that can be galvanized to raise funds. Moreover, incumbent MCs have the opportunity to sponsor and support legislation that is beneficial to their districts, and they can tout this legislative record and their other accomplishments during a reelection campaign. The work that they have been able to do while in Congress helps to solidify support among the voters, who usually return the incumbent to office as many times as he or she decides to run.

In politics, however, there are no absolutes, and Joe Schwarz was facing a difficult situation in seeking reelection in 2006. Schwarz had won his party's 2004 primary with only 28 percent of the vote—the remaining 72 percent had been split among five conservative candidates. It wasn't hard to see that if only one or two conservatives had run in that primary, the moderate Schwarz probably would have lost. Given a narrower field in the conservative Seventh District, Dr. Schwarz would have gone to Washington as a tourist rather than as a congressman.

The Schwarz team learned in November 2005 that they would have a political struggle on their hands in the bid to win reelection to the House of Representatives. Tim Walberg—evangelical pastor, former state legislator, and recent unsuccessful congressional candidate—announced that he was going to challenge Congressman Schwarz in the Republican primary

Congressman Schwarz surrounded by supporters during a campaign speech in early 2006. The push for reelection began earlier than usual because of the primary challenge from Tim Walberg, and it quickly turned ugly.

the following August. As any serious challenger would do, Walberg went to work gathering support and money.

The campaign season began gaining momentum in the spring. One of the surest signs that electoral politics was becoming the focus for at least some members of the Schwarz operation came in March, when Matt Marsden took a leave from his position as chief of staff to manage the congressman's reelection campaign. Also, Louie Meizlish left Washington to come back to the district, and Paul Egnatuk left his post in the Battle Creek office to work on the campaign. All three were switched from the congressional payroll to the campaign payroll; when they went "on leave" from their jobs with the federal government, contributions to their 401K accounts ceased, and they were permitted to keep their health insurance only if they made monthly out-of-pocket payments.

In April, an article in the *Lansing State Journal* carried the headline "Race for Schwarz's Seat Begins in Earnest."[1] It was an early start for a

House campaign, particularly one featuring an incumbent. Ordinarily, neither the people nor the media pay much attention at this stage to congressional elections, especially midterm elections that lack the accompanying drama of a presidential race. Typically, campaigns for the House of Representatives first become visible during summer parades, street fairs, and festivals, and the biggest push comes between Labor Day and election day. But this pattern speaks to general election politics, not primaries. Competitive primaries in an incumbent MC's own party are rare, so Michigan's Seventh District was already a bit extraordinary. Because the primary election was to take place in August, the campaigns had to establish their own timetables, and the *Journal* article predicted an intense campaign over the next four months.

The article also gave a sense of what the campaign would be about. The Walberg campaign's strategy was to paint Schwarz as a liberal, out of touch with the voters of the Seventh District. Walberg was going to hammer hard on the hottest of the hot-button issues for the religious right—namely, abortion. In April, his campaign ran radio advertisements criticizing Schwarz's position on abortion and trumpeting the endorsement Walberg had received from Right to Life of Michigan. The article in the Lansing paper also suggested that voters would be wise to expect a costly campaign: "The race is certain to be expensive. The conservative Club for Growth Political Action Committee is backing Walberg and has created a special Web site, joeschwarzisaliberal.com. The moderate Republican Main Street Partnership is expected to run radio and television ads on Schwarz's behalf." [2]

Less than two weeks later, the race for the Republican nomination in the Seventh District was again a top story in the *Lansing State Journal.* This time the headline proclaimed, "Walberg Camp's Cash Race Outpacing Schwarz," and the accompanying article stated that in the first quarter of 2006, Walberg had raised $179,361, while Schwarz reportedly had raised $153,873. [3] In addition, the paper noted that 70 percent of Walberg's total cash came from members of the Club for Growth.

The race was already becoming nasty. Among the charges leveled against Schwarz by the Club for Growth was that his score on the National Taxpayers Union's survey of lawmakers' fiscal conservatism was quite low. They also criticized his opposition to drilling for oil in ANWR and his support for Medicare coverage of Viagra prescriptions. Of the right-wing advocacy group's aggressive campaign against the congressman, Schwarz campaign spokesman John Truscott said, "It's personal, it's not based on policy. ... He [Schwarz] beat them last time, they were stung by it and they made him a target."[4]

Both candidates began the time-honored tradition of picking up endorsements from high-profile supporters. As the incumbent, Congressman Schwarz was in a better position to gain the public support of prominent Republicans such as Michigan's former governor, John Engler, who endorsed him as early as March. Throughout the spring, Joe also gained the endorsements of a number of influential party members at the national level, including House Majority Leader John Boehner, House Armed Services Committee chair Duncan Hunter, Senator John McCain, and President George W. Bush, as well as a host of local Republicans, including Clark Bisbee and Gene DeRossett, who had run against Schwarz and Walberg in the '04 primary. (The other Republicans involved in that race did not endorse either candidate in the 2006 primary contest.) Schwarz also picked up endorsements from the larger newspapers in the district as well as from a varied list of interest groups—labor unions, teachers unions, the National Rifle Association, the League of Conservation Voters, and, of course, the Main Street Partnership. Walberg's endorsements included several conservative members of the Michigan state legislature in addition to the Club for Growth PAC and Right to Life of Michigan.

By May, the campaign strategies of both candidates had become very clear. Schwarz was running on his record, as the campaign slogan displayed on billboards along I-94 proclaimed: *Congressman Joe Schwarz— Real Representation, Real Results.* The Walberg strategy was to paint Joe Schwarz as a liberal whose values were not in step with those of voters in the district.

As a means to emphasize the congressman's record, the Schwarz team circulated *The Schwarz for Congress Report* to a broad Internet population in May. The report had two basic purposes: to herald the congressman's first-term accomplishments, and to suggest where the Walberg campaign was playing fast and loose with the truth. The report began by noting that Schwarz had played a pivotal role in saving the National Guard base, and the jobs connected to it, in Battle Creek, and then emphasized that he had secured hundreds of thousands of dollars for road repairs on I-94 and U.S. 12—two major east-west thoroughfares in the Seventh District. Next was a section entitled, "On Taxes, Tort Reform and Fiscal Responsibility," which contained five bulleted statements noting that Schwarz had voted for the extension of the president's tax cuts; for repeal of the "death tax"; for the Stealth Tax Relief Act, aimed at saving middle-class individuals and families from higher taxes; for the Lawsuit Reduction Act; and for the Deficit Reduction Act.

The second part of the report was more combatively titled "Setting the Record Straight." It began with the accusation that "Walberg and his cynical financial backers in Washington have consistently avoided addressing the real issues Congress deals with. Instead, they focus their negative dialog on social issues better handled by state governments. ..." After charging that Walberg's rhetoric was often inconsistent, the piece concluded by noting that while Walberg was a member, and later chairman, of the Michigan House Appropriations Subcommittee on Corrections, $500,000 was allocated for workout facilities for prisoners and $200,000 was appropriated for electronic law libraries in correctional facilities. The report also asserted that Walberg had voted against requiring prisoners who earned money in prison to pay restitution to their crime victims.

In June, the Schwarz team distributed a second Internet report, this one entitled *Fact Check '06: Correcting Preacher Tim Walberg's Misrepresentations and Lies.* This report began with a section called "Background and Clarification," explaining that "Club for Growth is not a 'think tank' or a 'public policy group' as it is sometimes characterized. ... It is a political hatchet team that raises millions to buy elections." The report continued, charging that the Club "has bundled hundreds of thousands of dollars in contributions from non-Michigan residents to support Tim Walberg's campaign. ... Tim Walberg and CFG are tied at the hip. ... Their talking points are the same (visit www.clubforgrowth.org and www.walbergforcongress.com). Any notion that the Club for Growth ads are 'issue ads' not tied to campaigning is patently false." [5]

It's hard to believe, but it's

TRUE!

Liberal Congressman Joe Schwarz voted to use your tax dollars to pay for Viagra for welfare recipients.
Source: House Vote 312, 2005

But Schwarz's liberal record of wasting your tax dollars didn't stop with taxpayer funded Viagra.

Schwarz also voted to use your tax dollars to pay for a swimming pool in California, an Aquarium in Connecticut, and even a Bridge to Nowhere in Alaska.
Source: House Vote 277 (2006), House Vote 298 (2006), House Vote 65 (2005)

That's not just liberal, it's **SHAMEFUL.**

CALL JOE SCHWARZ AT 517-783-4486 AND TELL HIM TO
change his shamefully liberal record of wasting our tax dollars.

The *"Viagra" ad run by the Walberg camp seemed to kick off the "RINO" hunt, painting Schwarz as a "liberal" who was happy to sponsor irresponsible spending bills. Schwarz countered that he supported Medicare and Medicaid spending on Sidenafil (marketed as Viagra) because it is also used to treat children with pulmonary hypertension.*

Fact Check '06 also took on the issue of the "liberal" label that the Walberg campaign had hung on Schwarz, pointing out that conservative bulwarks such as President Bush and Speaker of the House Dennis Hastert, who had endorsed Schwarz in the primary battle, were certainly not likely to support liberals. In addition, the piece spoke to several other claims made by Walberg and the Club for Growth, including the accusation that Congressman Schwarz had voted to spend tax dollars to support the use of Viagra. In fact, it explained, Schwarz had opposed an amendment to ban Medicare and Medicaid payments for Viagra because the drug Sidenafil, which is marketed as Viagra, is also used to treat pulmonary hypertension in children.

During the spring and summer, the congressman returned to the district as often as possible, although, as it happened, he had to be in Washington five days a week for votes much of the time and so had to pack as much as he could into weekend visits. Often, the Schwarz staff scheduled Joe's weekends around participation, at a hectic pace, in the annual summer events in towns throughout the district. There was at least one parade every weekend, and sometimes more, as part of these summer events with names that ring of the Midwest—the Jackson Rose Parade, Grand Ledge Yankee Doodle Days, and the Cereal Festival in Joe's hometown, Battle Creek. At the Cereal Festival, which ran for three days in June, one of the major events was the annual staging of the world's longest breakfast table, at which the local companies, Kellogg and Post, feed breakfast to as many people as show up. This is the kind of event that a hometown congressman certainly would not miss.

The summer season was broken up by two congressional recesses—one at Memorial Day and the other at the Fourth of July—and these periods were booked with meetings and fund-raisers as well as tours of local businesses. Congressman Schwarz held some forums for business and community leaders, highlighting participation by Commerce Secretary Gutierrez at one and by former House Speaker Newt Gingrich at another. The campaign staff would have liked to have had Joe for appearances seven days a week, so, not surprisingly, he was kept very busy whenever he was home.

In July, a *Detroit News* story called the Schwarz-Walberg race the most contentious congressional primary election in Michigan.[6] The article made mention of Schwarz's impressive array of endorsements but suggested that the race was the "ripest" in the state for an upset. The story noted that Walberg was backed by both the national and Michigan Right to Life organizations, as well as by the Club for Growth, which "has flooded the airwaves with messages calling Schwarz 'outrageously liberal.'" Schwarz's reaction to the liberal label—"It's pretty amusing because if one looks at my voting record, it's pretty much pure vanilla Republican"—was quoted, and the article noted that the Michigan Chamber of Commerce agreed with Schwarz. "Its president, Jim Barrett, is featured in radio ads saying: 'Don't take seriously the claim by a few that Joe Schwarz is some kind of a flaming liberal. He scored 88 percent on the U.S. Chamber's voting record on business and tax issues.'"[7]

The candidates' issue positions were also detailed in the *News* article. With respect to the auto industry, which obviously is critical to Michigan, Schwarz spoke about the need for Congress and the Bush administration to address the problem of China's and Japan's currency manipulation, which subsidizes their products and forces U.S. goods out of the market. Walberg, on the other hand, spoke of reducing the tax burden on American companies. On Iraq, Schwarz recalled that he had been part of a group that met with the president and urged him to impress upon the Iraqi government that the U.S. commitment there would not be open-ended, that at some point the United States would leave. "Historians will debate the wisdom of initiating this fight in Iraq," Schwarz said, "but we are there, and if at all possible, we must finish the job." Walberg took a more militant position: "President Bush was correct to remove a terrorist-sponsoring, America-hating, WMD-possessing, oil-rich murderous dictator from power. …our troops are fighting a necessary battle and they and the mission need our support."

On the issue of Social Security, Walberg favored privatization, while Schwarz said his top priority was keeping Social Security solvent. A constitutional amendment to ban same-sex marriage was supported by Walberg, while Schwarz indicated that he did not support gay marriage but thought the issue was better-suited to state-level decision making. Walberg opposed abortion; Schwarz voiced a personal opposition to abortion along with an absolute unwillingness to support overturning the Supreme Court's 1973 *Roe v. Wade* decision.[8]

On July 20, less than three weeks before the August 8 primary election, the Associated Press carried a story from Washington with the headline, "Schwarz Campaign Files FEC Complaint against Walberg."[9] The complaint charged that Walberg and Club for Growth had coordinated campaign activities—a violation of federal campaign finance laws. Under the law, "issue advocacy" or partisan groups, called 527s (after the provision in the tax code that refers to them), are prohibited from coordinating expenditures with a candidate's campaign organization. The following day, the Schwarz campaign produced a press release detailing the charges and noting, in particular, that Walberg's campaign had bought poll results from the Club for Growth and had coordinated activities involving research and advertising buys.[10] The battle between the Schwarz and Walberg campaigns was becoming more heated every day.

Moderate candidates such as Joe Schwarz were having a tough time in the 2006 primary season. "With control of Congress on the line this November," observed the authors of an article that ran in *Newsweek* during the first week in August, "both political parties are pressing the wedge issues—immigration, stem-cell research and, most prominently, Iraq.

And creatures of the center are struggling to simply stay in the game."[11] Among the candidates featured in the article were Republican Senator Mike DeWine of Ohio, Senator Joe Lieberman, a Democrat from Connecticut, and Congressman Joe Schwarz of Michigan.

As the election drew near, it was a rare day that residents in Michigan's Seventh District did not receive several pieces of mail supporting one or another of the candidates. The Walberg ads were largely negative, leveling accusations against Joe Schwarz that included spending tax dollars for prescription Viagra, supporting higher taxes, favoring raising taxes on gasoline, and justifying government's use of the power of eminent domain to take an individual's home and give it to a private developer. The brochures rarely missed an opportunity to attach the word *liberal* to Schwarz's record. A majority of the Walberg mail came from Club for Growth. Of all the mail sent by the "Walberg for Congress" campaign, the most positive was a "Dear Neighbor" piece from Sue Walberg, the candidate's wife, who extolled her husband's past service in the public arena and his commitment to family values, testifying that he was a great father and husband, and a person of integrity. This particular bit of campaign literature featured a picture of Tim and Sue Walberg, along with a dog, against a backdrop that evoked a rural setting.

Campaign ads for Congressman Schwarz were slightly more varied in tone. Some pieces were completely positive, heralding the congressman's demonstrated common sense and compassionate leadership, or publicizing his role in the successful fight to keep open the Air National Guard base in Battle Creek. Other brochures described Schwarz as a "Ronald Reagan fiscal conservative," noting that he had been the recipient of the "Hero of the Taxpayer Award" from the Americans for Tax Reform and trumpeting his endorsement by President Bush. Also, the American Medical Association Political Action Committee (AMPAC) sent mail in support of Dr. Schwarz, noting his efforts to enact medical liability insurance reform and his support of tort reform, which would cap the amount of money awarded in medical malpractice lawsuits.

The Schwarz campaign's literature also offered plenty of negative content as well. One ad featured a quotation from the *Detroit News*, charging that Walberg was one of the "least effective legislators in Lansing." This

The Walberg team ran positive ads emphasizing the candidate's family life and his prior political commitments (above) as well as a series of negative attack ads claiming that Schwarz had voted for millions of dollars in "pork barrel spending" (left).

Our Congressman Joe Schwarz
has a Proven Record of Serving Us!

Tim Walberg Failed Us!

Joe Schwarz

Tim Walberg

Hero of the Taxpayer

TOP TEN WORST

Joe Schwarz was recently presented with the "Hero of the Taxpayer Award" by Americans for Tax Reform.

(Source: Gongwer News Article, Michigan, June 8, 2006)

Joe Schwarz – Voted for Tax Cuts!
Joe Schwarz put taxpayers first by voting for President Bush's tax cuts, helping us keep more of our hard-earned money.
(Source: HR 4297, November, 2005)

Helping Create and Save Jobs for Us!
"Schwarz was instrumental in the BRAC decision to overturn the original Pentagon recommendation to close the Battle Creek Air National Guard Base and transfer the 110th Fighter Wing to Selfridge."
(Source: The Detroit News, 8-30-05)

Solving Problems and Making Sure We Get Our Share of Federal Dollars!
Joe Schwarz brought home much needed federal dollars to fix I-94 and improve our quality of life here at home.
(Source: HR 3, July, 2005)

As a State Legislator in Lansing, Tim Walberg was named one of the 10 Worst State Legislators.
(Source: The Detroit News, 9/11/88)

Walberg Supports a National Sales Tax
(Source: Battle Creek Enquirer, 7/5/06)
This national sales tax will raise our taxes and hurt Michigan's economy.

Voting Against Jobs We Need
Tim Walberg voted "no" on creating 5,800 local good paying jobs.
(Sources: Roll Call 285, 4/4/95 & Roll Calls 874-881, 11/20/96)

The Schwarz team also ran both positive and negative ads. In one broadside, Schwarz claimed the mantle of a "Reagan Republican" and drew attention to his endorsement by prominent party leaders in order to emphasize his moderation and trustworthiness (left). The negative ads (above) highlighted Walberg's citation among the "Top Ten Worst" state legislators, as reported by the Detroit News.

Congressman Joe Schwarz –
a Ronald Reagan Republican and Fiscal Conservative Our Families Can Trust!

Endorsed for Re-Election by
President George W. Bush
– Our President!

mailer then went on to provide other unflattering assessments of Walberg that had been offered by the *News* while he was a member of the state legislature.

The barrage of mail from both campaigns was designed to keep the candidates' names before the voters, and it made the race in Michigan's Seventh District very expensive. Anyone reading the *Detroit News* on July 30, 2006, knew that Schwarz was in a tight race. In "A Good Man Fights for His Political Life," Nolan Finley began his Sunday editorial with the statement, "I can't believe it. My old friend Joe Schwarz is a big, fat liberal." Finley's piece reflected his admiration for the congressman, noting that Schwarz was difficult to label, and that while he, Finley, did not always agree with Joe's positions, he regarded Schwarz as a commonsense, pragmatic politician who stood by his convictions and should be reelected.[12]

On primary election night, the Schwarz campaign was back at Schuler's Restaurant in Marshall, Michigan. The downstairs party room again featured food and drink, a podium adorned by a "Schwarz for Congress" sign, balloons, campaign paraphernalia, and all the usual trappings. Key staffers once more gathered in an upstairs conference room—though it was a different room from the one that had been used on election night 2004. This war room had a small lobby outside the main room and a small office off the waiting area where the congressman could go to escape the tumult. The mood was anxious. Everyone who had worked on the campaign expected a tight race, much like the primary two years earlier that had ended in celebration.

Matt Marsden again stood at the head of the table, huddled with another hired pro, Richard Czuba. The "campaign kids"—as Rebecca Schneider, the congressman's district director, affectionately referred to a group of young campaign staffers—were seated along the sides of the table with their laptops. The room was very orderly, exhibiting none of the loosely organized chaos that usually characterizes an election night war room. "Actually," Rebecca recounted,

> …it was kind of eerie. There was a weird energy in the room. … I didn't want to be in there. It was pretty clear that if you were not directly involved

with gathering election returns, you were not welcome in there. It was tense. As the numbers came in, it grew more tense, and it became clear that the folks inside the war room did not want noise or distraction nearby. They wanted someone to sit by the stairs and sort of serve as a gatekeeper, to be nice and firm in telling people to go back down to the party and not hang around the area. I became that person.

Rebecca's evocation of the scene at Schuler's continued: "The press gets very anxious and a little pushy as the 11:00 p.m. news period approaches. They want their story well before 11:00, and we simply were not ready to give them a story by that time. But I could see in Matt's face, and in the boss's face, that things were not going well. . . ."

As the evening wore on, the congressman spent more time in the office off the lobby of the war room. From time to time, he would ask to see someone. Rebecca was asked to get Joe's daughter, Brennan, and they talked for a while. Some local judges also stopped in to see Joe, as did some community power brokers who had helped on the campaign. Sometime between 9:00 and 10:00 p.m., Congressman Schwarz wanted to go down and speak to his supporters, to let them know that the returns were not looking particularly good. Matt seemed opposed to the idea, viewing it as a way of wallowing in bad news twice. Rebecca thought that perhaps Joe wanted to allow people to leave before he conceded the election, as if a smaller crowd might make it easier somehow. Others speculated that Joe's medical training was kicking in—that he was feeling as though he ought to prep the patient for surgery.

Eventually, Joe did go downstairs and indicated to the crowd his sense that things were not going well for the campaign. Soon after that, his cell phone rang, and Rebecca overheard a conversation that she assumed was with Senator McCain. "Well, John," the congressman said, "It looks like I'm going to lose." A short time later, Joe went downstairs again, and, flanked by his daughter and his chief of staff, conceded the race.

In the aftermath of the August primary, a fair amount was written about the difficulties that political moderates faced in their bids for reelection. A *USA Today* story interpreted the primary election defeats of both Joe Lieberman and Joe Schwarz as a signal that candidates who failed to play to their party's base did so at their own risk and the conservative-leaning *Washington Times* made a similar argument.[13] Of course, this observation was completely in keeping with another piece of conventional wisdom—that in strongly partisan districts, an incumbent viewed as vulnerable should expect a stiff primary challenge.[14] Given the split that characterized the Republican Party in 2006—pitting the moderate element of the party against a more conservative far-right wing— Walberg's challenge and ultimate success could not be considered a great surprise. That Joe Schwarz managed to do as well as he did in the face of a well-financed and -targeted single challenger actually suggests, ironically, that he had expanded his base of support considerably since the 2004 primary.

The final vote tally of the Republican primary in Michigan's Seventh District was 53 percent (33, 244 votes) for Walberg and 47 percent (29, 349 votes) for Schwarz. Joe was disappointed by the turnout, which was less than 15 percent in his own home county, and less than 20 percent district-wide. "It's a classic case of a well-organized, single-issue bloc winning a low-turnout election," he observed. "Anybody who studies elections, and understands them, knows that well-organized, aggressive minorities do well in low-turnout elections." Matt Marsden was a bit less circumspect about the connection of the religious right to the Walberg victory. Believing that many of those who support the Club for Growth have a strong social agenda, and that it was those hot-button issues— abortion, gay rights, and gun control—that galvanized the Walberg voters, Matt vehemently proclaimed: "They are zealots who would like to see everybody who doesn't agree with them put in a camp with the gate locked. I'm guessing a lot of people woke up after the election and said 'Holy shit, maybe I should have gotten out and voted.'"

On September 17, 2006, Congressman Schwarz reflected on his defeat in the Sunday edition of the *Washington Post,* beginning, "I am the political equivalent of a woolly mammoth, a rarity headed for extinction. ... Yes, I'm a moderate." Schwarz acknowledged that he had been beaten by voter apathy and by well-organized, well-funded "moral absolutist" groups. He voiced his concern for the political center, noting that "fewer and fewer sensible...candidates will have any chance of being elected," although "politics needs a middle" for effective public policymaking.

"Somehow, some way," Joe concluded, "moderates must understand that they will go the way of the moa, the dodo, and, appropriately, the woolly mammoth unless they learn to fight as hard for the policies of the sane and rational center as the far right and far left fight for the extremes."[15]

When asked to reflect on his term in Congress, Schwarz noted his frustration with the group dynamic of the House Republicans. "There was no cohesive Republican Party," he observed. "It's very balkanized...North vs. South, religious right vs. moderates. There's very little sense of 'What's best for the country?' In many ways, it's reminiscent of the Democratic Party of the late 1950s and 60s, when southern Democrats were so far removed from the rest of the party." Joe continued, "You know, there are a good many Americans who are moderate, many in both parties, but there is no way to make them cohesive. Many believe that this country needs a third party, a middle party, but it would certainly take a seismic political event for that to happen."

The congressman took some comfort in comments made to him when he returned to Washington after the primary. Duncan Hunter, chairman of the House Armed Services Committee, bemoaned Joe's loss, saying, "Gee, Joe, I got 62 members of this committee with far too few combat veterans...you show up and I'm delighted...another combat veteran. And you have to go and lose...this does not make me happy." Bob Goodlatte, chair of the House Agriculture Committee, offered similar sentiments: "I finally get someone with an interest in and an understanding of veterinary medicine issues, and then I lose him...isn't that just great." Joe was gratified to know that both of these legislators had valued his participation as a member of their committees.

Joe Schwarz was not happy ending his electoral career with a loss in the primary. "I'm a graceful loser," he said, "but not a good one. I'm just not sure what I'll do long-term. For now, I'll practice medicine.... I'm already back to a day of surgery a week, but ...."

Again, Matt Marsden was less philosophical: "We never thought we were a lock.... We knew our '04 victory was the result of all of those conservatives splitting up the right-wing vote." But he was not shy about placing blame for the low turnout that contributed to his candidate's loss in 2006:

I worked hard to impress upon organized labor and the teachers that while I realized that they were not quick to endorse a Republican, Schwarz was clearly their best hope, and that Walberg was basically against everything they stood for. They made clear commitments to us that they would marshal their troops and get out the vote. Labor failed us and did not live up to their commitments. ... The MEA [Michigan Education Association] failed us—13,000 people we communicated with and their leadership assured us they would get out their vote, and they just did not turn out. Main Street did not deliver as they promised they would. They promised to do television ads to counter Club for Growth's early ads, and I hounded them to get their pro-Schwarz stuff on the air, and they kept telling me, it's on its way. Yeah, well, when it arrived, more than a month after they promised, it was too little too late. ... All of these groups should be kicking themselves everyday. Walberg did not win...apathy and disinterest won. We'll be back. ...

At those final words, the events of the past two years flashed by in my mind, and I found myself wondering...was Joe Schwarz just taking some time off between his freshman and sophomore terms?

Postscript

Election Day: November 7, 2006

ELECTION DAY 2006 brought an all-day rain to Michigan's Seventh District. As she had done before, Sharon Renier provided the Democratic Party opposition to the heavily favored Republican in a general election campaign that, once again, was far less visible than the primary election campaign.

Again, Renier's campaign was underfunded, while the Club for Growth had continued its mail campaign in support of Tim Walberg's candidacy, producing at least five different pieces that reached households with increasing frequency as election day drew near. The Walberg campaign itself sent out a piece claiming that Renier would support gay marriage and another proclaiming, "If you support liberal values, Sharon Renier is on your side." There was also a flyer that featured a photo of the candidate and his wife, affirming that Walberg was committed to protecting "traditional values."

However, if you looked closely, you could see that this general election differed from the one that had sent Joe Schwarz to Congress two years earlier. This time around, the *Battle Creek Enquirer* bemoaned Schwarz's loss in the primary and, somewhat surprisingly, endorsed Renier in the general, noting that Walberg had taken too many positions with which the paper's editorial staff disagreed.[1] *The Ann Arbor News* did not endorse either candidate.

The biggest news story of the election cycle broke in late October, when it became public information that a Walberg campaign staffer had been arrested on charges of child abuse and had pleaded guilty. The staffer had remained on the Walberg payroll after the candidate learned of the situation but resigned after the story made the local papers. As election day approached, there was talk of a possible "Schwarz effect" that could bring moderates to support Renier.

In the end, however, the Michigan Seventh was not one of the nearly thirty seats that the Democrats won that day to gain majority status in the House. Tim Walberg received 51 percent of the vote to Renier's 46 percent. The new congressman's freshman orientation would begin in mid-November 2006.

Notes

Prologue

1. See Edward I. Sidlow, *Challenging the Incumbent: An Underdog's Undertaking* (Washington, D.C.: CQ Press, 2004). This behind-the-scenes story of the 2000 race in Illinois' Eighth Congressional District documents the day-to-day dynamics of a political contest in which a young challenger takes on a longtime incumbent.

Chapter 1

1. Associated Press, "Candidates Try to Distinguish Themselves as Primary Nears," June 30, 2004, at www.Mlive.com.

2. Eric J. Greene, "Expensive GOP Primary Features in 7th," *Battle Creek Enquirer*, July 25, 2004, sec. 2, pp. 1–5.

3. Chris Andrews, "7th District Rivals Offer Spending Platforms," *Lansing State Journal*, July 6, 2004, B1.

4. Owen G. Abbe et al., "Are Professional Campaigns More Negative?" in *Playing Hardball: Campaigning for the U.S. Congress,* ed. Paul S. Herrnson (Upper Saddle River, N.J.: Prentice Hall, 2001), 86.

5. Brett Thomas, "Was Nick Smith Offered a Bribe?" December 5, 2003, at http://www.woodtv.com/Global/story.asp?S=1553300&nav=0RcdJW5I.

6. Brian Wheeler, "The Candidates," *Jackson Citizen Patriot*, August 1, 2004, A1.

Chapter 2

1. Paul S. Herrnson, *Congressional Elections: Campaigning at Home and in Washington,* 3rd ed. (Washington D.C.: CQ Press, 2000), 181.

2. "RMSP Mission," www.republicanmainstreet.org/mission _temp.htm.

3. All three candidates' remarks were quoted in Chris Gautz, *Adrian Daily Telegram,* October 5, 2004.

4. Ibid.

5. Ibid.

6. "The City of New Orleans," 1970, 1971 EMI U Catalogue, Inc., and Turnpike Tom Music (ASCAP).

7. "Schwarz Has Experience Needed for Congress," *Ann Arbor News,* October 13, 2004, available at www.Mlive.com/columns/aanews.

8. *Delta Waverly Community News,* October 24, 2004, at www.hometown-life.com/Delta/News (accessed 10/24/06).

9. "Enquirer's View," October 24, 2004, at www.battlecreekenquirer.com/.

Chapter 3

1. Memo from Rev. Daniel P. Coughlin, Office of the Chaplain, U.S. House of Representatives, Washington, D.C.

2. Congressional Management Foundation, www.cmfweb.org/Aboutus.asp; *Setting Course: A Congressional Management Guide,* 9th ed. (Washington, D.C.: CMF, 2004), xviii.

3. Robert H. Salisbury and Kenneth A. Shepsle, "U.S. Congressman as Enterprise," *Legislative Studies Quarterly* 6, no. 4 (November 1981): 559. Interestingly, during the same time period, the numbers of presidential staff grew dramatically as well.

Chapter 4

1. Roger H. Davidson and Walter J. Oleszek, *Congress and Its Members,* 10th ed. (Washington, D.C.: CQ Press, 2006), 193.

2. John Kingdon, *Congressmen's Voting Decisions* (New York: Harper & Row, 1973).

3. Quoted in Katherine Hutt Scott, "Area Lawmakers Respond to Address," *Battle Creek Enquirer,* February 3, 2005.

4. Quoted in "Conservative Group Targets Michigan Representative, Other Republicans Considered on the Fence," *Detroit Free Press,* February 4, 2005.

5. Quoted in Brian Wheeler, "Ad Targets Schwarz for Support," *Jackson Citizen Patriot,* February 9, 2005.

6. Kingdon, *Congressmen's Voting Decisions,* 22.

7. Standing committees in the House and Senate have staffs that are separate from members' personal staffs. Committee staff positions tend to be more stable than personal staff positions and, in general, are better paid. Typically, a committee has both clerical staffers, who deal with mail and work with documents produced by the committee, and professional staff members, who are often lawyers with expertise in the committee's substantive policy area.

8. It is not uncommon for congressmen and congresswomen to conduct such polls during the year. It should be noted that these efforts are paid for with campaign funds rather than official congressional funds.

Chapter 5

1. Stewart, J., concurring opinion, *Jacobellis v. Ohio,* 378 v. Ohio (1964).

2. For an early and frequently cited attempt to explain how representation works, based on a study of legislators in four states, see John C. Wahlke, Heinz Eulau, William Buchanan, and LeRoy C. Ferguson, *The Legislative System: Explorations in Legislative Behavior* (New York: John Wiley and Sons, 1962), 267–286.

3. As scholars continued to grapple with the concept of representation, they examined how congressional votes on issues matched up with public opinion in the district. In other words, they wanted to know if a member of Congress was acting in a way that was commensurate with public opinion back home. The answer, they found, was "sometimes." It depended on the issue and its salience in the district. See, for example, Warren E. Miller and Donald E. Stokes, "Constituency Influence in Congress," *American Political Science Review* 57 (1963): 45–56.

4. Robert Weissberg, "Collective vs. Dyadic Representation in Congress," *American Political Science Review* 72 (1978): 535–547. For additional discussion, see Patricia A. Hurley, "Collective Representation Reappraised," *Legislative Studies Quarterly* 7 (1982): 119–136.

5. The following discussion is drawn from Morris P. Fiorina, *Congress: Keystone of the Washington Establishment* (New Haven: Yale University Press, 1977), 41–46.

6. Quoted in Liz Ruskin, "A.N.W.R. Opponents Rally against Defense Bill Strategy," *Rutland Herald,* December 17, 2005, accessed at www.RutlandHerald.com.

7. "Schwarz Applauded for Stand," *Jackson Citizen Patriot,* December 8, 2005, accessed at www.citpat.com.

8. See Roger H. Davidson and Walter J. Oleszek, *Congress and Its Members,* 8th ed. (Washington, D.C.: CQ Press, 2002), 380.

9. For a discussion of the importance of constituent casework to the electoral process, see Fiorina, *Congress: Keystone of the Washington Establishment,* 45–48.

10. The following discussion is based on David R. Mayhew, *Congress: The Electoral Connection* (New Haven: Yale University Press, 1974), 49–77.

11. U.S. senators have been directly elected only since the ratification of the Seventeenth Amendment in 1913. Before that time, they were chosen by their respective state legislatures, as directed in the Constitution.

Chapter 7

1. The House Republican Conference is composed of all members of the Republican Party in the House of Representatives. It serves as the forum for electing party leaders at the start of each new Congress and meets to discuss party policy and legislative issues.

2. Editorial, "Upton, Schwarz Deserve Praise For Stem-Cell Vote," *Kalamazoo Gazette,* April 27, 2005, at http://www. Kalamazoo-Gazette.com.

3. Barbara Walters, "Fight Gears Up for Fed Center," *Kalamazoo Gazette,* April 23, 2005, at http://www. Kalamazoo-Gazette.com.

4. George Weeks, "Joe Schwarz Was Key Figure in Easing State Base Closings," *Detroit News,* August 30, 2005, at http://www.detnews.com.

Chapter 8

1. Chris Andrews, "Race for Schwarz's Seat Begins in Earnest," *Lansing State Journal,* April 11, 2006, at http://www.LSJ.com.

2. Ibid.

3. Faith Bremner, "Walberg Camp's Cash Race Outpacing Schwarz," *Lansing State Journal*, April 19, 2006, at http://www.LSJ.com.

4. Ibid.

5. *Fact Check '06*, June 20, 2006, at http://www.schwarzforcongress.com.

6. Charlie Cain, "Social Issues Stoke Race in West Mich.," *Detroit News*, July 17, 2006, at http://www.detnews.com.

7. Ibid.

8. Ibid.

9. Ken Thomas, "Schwarz Campaign Files FEC Complaint against Walberg," *Associated Press*, July 20, 2006, at http://www.ap.org.

10. Press Release, "Walberg Campaign in Violation," July 21, 2006, at http://www.media.schwarzforcongress.com.

11. Jonathan Darman and Holly Bailey, "A Gang under Siege," *Newsweek*, August 7, 2006, 37.

12. Nolan Finley, "A Good Man Fights for His Political Life," *Detroit News*, July 30, 2006.

13. "Fate of Two Joes Reflects Drive for Partisan Purity," *USA Today*, August 9, 2006, at http://www.usatoday.com; Amy Fagan and Stephen Dinan, "Schwarz's Loss Seen as Cautionary Tale," *Washington Times*, August 14, 2006, at http://www.washingtontimes.com.

14. See Peter F. Galderisi et al., eds., *Congressional Primaries and the Politics of Representation* (Lanham, Md.: Rowman and Littlefield, 2001), 5–6.

15. Joe Schwarz, "Don't Lose Like Me," *Washington Post*, September 17, 2006, at http://www.washingtonpost.com.

Postscript

1. Editorial, *Battle Creek Enquirer*, October 31, 2006, at http://www.battlecreekenquirer.com.

Index